Out of My MIND

THE ART OF CREATIVITY

by

KAREN M. WEIHS

AUTHOR:	Karen M. Weihs
ART & PAINTINGS:	Karen M. Weihs
KAREN WEIHS PHOTO:	Ervin Jackson
FRONT COVER:	H. Donald Kroitzsh
EDITOR:	Tish Lynn
ASSOCIATE EDITOR:	Patrick Grafton
LAYOUT:	H. Donald Kroitzsh

Printed in the United States

Published by:
Five Corners Publications, Ltd.
5052 Route 100
Plymouth, Vermont 05056   USA

Out of My Mind
ISBN: 1-886699-20-8

ACKNOWLEDGMENTS

I express my gratitude to **Tish Lynn**, a superior editor; and to my novelist friend, **Patrick Grafton**, and his wife, **Diana**, for editorial support; **Gil Shuler**; my sister, **Lynn McDaniel** for typing; my many, many **friends** too numerous to mention, but you know who you are — along with many other talented and creative **friends at the Waterfront Gallery**.

FOREWORD

This book was born out of sharing. Through teaching and being taught, I have learned that people who develop their creativity are more confident and courageous in life. Whether your profession is one of retail, medicine, service, writing, or the arts, pursuing your creative self will deepen your life and work experience.

Maybe you have a creative spirit, but you have had to suppress it because of life's demands, or maybe you feel you have lost it completely. Perhaps someone has told you there are more important things to do with your life than contemplate art, music or drama, or risk a new idea in business. You can heal your creative spirit by changing your attitude. If you open up your mind, your spirit will again be free to accept new goals, develop skills and enable your intuition to help guide you toward more creative behavior. Creativity needs cultivating, serenity and a support system. Your desire and your positive energy are essential. Years ago, I abandoned my fear of being creative to embrace a love for it. Through love, I became afraid not to be creative. Through love, I found the courage to bring every thought, every pain, and every fear with me — on the road to discovering my potential for creativity.

Together, let's explore how creativity can become a life force for you as it has been for me. If you become confident in your creativity, it will reward you. There is always risk involved, but the only failure is not trying. If you feel disconnected from yourself, and you are crying for the person you used to be, maybe the inner child, that lost spirit of youth; know that it takes a hurt to wake you up. Wake up, get up and get to work on your creative self. Creativity is not always sensible, but it is tantamount to personal happiness, therefore necessary.

Karen Weihs

The best part of one's life is the working part, the creative part. Believe me, I love to succeed… However the real spiritual and emotional excitement is in the doing.

Garson Kanin

DEDICATION

This book is dedicated to three special people: my sons **Tyson** and **Justin** and my husband **Chris**. **Justin** has the best creative attitude ever. His first whole sentence was "You can't make me," and I am sure it will be his last. He knows that his spirit is free, and he delights in himself and in turn delights others. **Tyson**, an intellectual, creative young man, is busy working in his own business to make his dream real. Both have learned the value of taking creative risks. My husband, **Chris** has inspired me, supported me, and given me the space and freedom to learn, grow, and fly. We share identities as creative partners, enjoying the energy we bring to each other's lives.

"Once you make something real, it will travel without you."

Karen Weihs

KISS MY ART
AN   INTRODUCTION

When I was three, I learned that falling out of a moving automobile could hurt me. I'd been sitting in the back seat while my parents were busy having a conversation in the front when, all of a sudden, I opened the door and fell out. They drove nearly a mile before they'd noticed I was gone. By then, a local storekeeper, who'd seen the accident, was comforting me with some warm homemade biscuits. Ever since, biscuits have made me feel happy and safe. The familiar smell and taste of them make me want to create. They restore my soul when I'm feeling blue or fear that my creative soul has shriveled up. Somewhere deep inside of me I learned that day that life is fragile and unpredictable, and that we all need homemade biscuits to get us through. They became my Proustian "thé madeleine" — the key to unlocking my creative self. I have only to smell them or take a bite and I am instantly transported. The remembrance of sweetness past and the promise of more.

Each of us has these memory talismans that we carry around inside of us from other times, other places, other people. A taste, a smell, the sight of something can trigger the memory of a feeling or fear. Good or bad, these are the catalysts for our inspiration and creativity. Some choose to sublimate them or ignore them. Others are ignited by them and spend their lives trying to capture what they feel in words, dance, music, painting, invention, innovation, teaching, acting and flights of the imagination. The point is — we have a choice. We can all choose to exercise our creativity in whatever we do in life. We needn't be afraid of it, or feel that it is the exclusive domain of artists. We are all creative. The challenge is to let it flow through us and become an extension of our being in all that we do.

Creativity comes from the heart and the subconscious. Most of us are controlled by our thinking brain, the one that gets us up in the morning, makes us keep appointments, feeds us, dresses us, drives the car responsibly and balances the checkbook. When trying to get in touch with your creative *self*, you have to let go of your thinking brain and switch over to your artist brain, the part that is ignited by the heart; the part that thinks from the eyes down.

If you were driving a car with your artist brain, you'd never get where you were going. You'd be in endless accidents because of the visual and sensual distractions around you. You'd be writing poems in your head, concocting advertising jingles, imagining a painting, or composing an aria.

Finding the necessary balance between the thinking and artist brain is a constant challenge. What matters most is that you believe the value of your artist brain is equal to that of your thinking brain. Trust it, cultivate it and enjoy it and, one day, your reward will be the experience of working "out of your mind" — that is, out of your *thinking* mind and in your artist mind.

When did I know I was creative? Probably as a child when I drew my first picture, or made my first Halloween costume. All children instinctively know they are creative, but few of them grow up believing it. Some even turn away from it completely as adults, calling it frivolous and irresponsible. Only you can break through these perceptions for yourself. Only you can decide to stop saying "I can't do that well," or "I don't have time," or "Someday I'll make time for that," or "It's not important."

Don't wait another minute. Start scheduling your creative time just like chore time, family time, and exercise time. Do not undervalue it. Live your life according to what really matters to you and only you.

When did I know I was as artist? I remember exactly. It felt like the taste of a homemade biscuit. It felt like coming home. I was twenty-three, and I was painting an ibis, whose photo I had taken when living in Florida. I had been painting and drawing for quite some time and had a lot of work to show for it, but this was different. This time, it felt right. I felt like an artist, and I knew my true journey had begun.

Over the years, I was to take several detours — work, marriage and babies, not to mention the bouts of confusion, lack of confidence and hopelessness, but one particular event changed my life forever. Another car event. For some unexplainable reason, car crises have had a lot to do with my creative journey. This one occurred when I was fully grown. I was riding in the family car one rainy night when we lost control, and swerved to avoid a head-on collision, slamming right into a tree. Luckily, my two sons, my husband and I were all strapped in and survived.

As I lay in the hospital bed with neck and back injuries, an artist friend came to visit, and spoke words that would set me back on my journey as a painter and change my life forever.

"Life is short," he said. "Do what matters and what's important to you!"

In that moment, with the memory of facing death still fresh, I knew that I had to stop making excuses and taking detours, and dedicate my life to my journey as a painter.

Fortunately, I had the support of my family, but even if I hadn't, I would have had no choice. It had taken a brush with death for me to know in my heart what mattered most — to love my creative self and work.

Along the way I made a significant choice that kept the spark of my creative spirit alive. I chose to be positive. I chose to be inspired by the light in the world, rather than the dark. I refused to be overwhelmed by negativity, as many people are. Negativity discourages the urge to create, and sometimes destroys it.

You are a combination of experiences that happen to you and experiences you make happen. You cannot shut out the dark, difficult times in your life, but you can choose to use them rather than be consumed by them.

When you encounter negativity, remember the phrase— "Face it and replace it." Face your lack of confidence and replace it with hope. At first, it may seem hard, but with each confrontation, you will realize a more positive attitude, which will, in turn, put you in touch with your creative self.

My personal technique for facing it and replacing it involves visualization. When I experience negativity, I replace it with the image of something or someone I love and who loves me. This visualization reinforces my positive sense of self and purpose, dissolving the negativity.

However you do it, you must try to exorcise your negativity to enable your creative spirit to emerge. Because we are creatures of ritual and routine, try to come up with your own physical ritual of ridding yourself of negativity. One idea might be to write down all of the negative thoughts that plague you on individual slips of paper and burn them one by one, reducing them to ineffectual smoke. So much for their power over you. Or perhaps you might prefer to collect a small stone for every negative thought and throw each of them as far away from you as you can, or into the nearest river, pond or ocean.

Whatever you decide to do, make it something that you can routinely repeat, because negative thoughts crop up all the time, so be ready to exorcise them. Also, it might be helpful in your daily preparation to include a small, symbolic act that represents the exorcism and the freedom you feel. Light a match to symbolize the burning. Keep one stone/pebble that you turn over each day to symbolize the rejection of the old negative you. Symbols and rituals help us all to infuse meaning into our existence. Make your symbols and rituals positive, reinforcing ones, strong reminders of your potential and proof of each step along your journey.

Do not leave your journey to chance. Sit down and take the time to reflect on what you wish to accomplish and how.

When I was working as a master calligrapher, I received many commissions from corporations to produce hand-lettered mission statements for their conference areas. These statements were important to their professional image and to their employees' feeling of self-esteem, and it occurred to me that I should conceive a mission statement for myself, for my image, for my self-esteem, for my sense of purpose.

Establish your own mission statement with clear goals and a personal vision. Write it down and up-date it often.

Here is mine:

MISSION STATEMENT

1. *Karen Weihs, artist* serves two unique client groups.

   a. <u>Self</u>: The business of art requires cultivating. *Karen Weihs, artist*, will agree to take classes, attend seminars, read trade magazines and books to educate her mind, and ease her skill power into professionalism. *Karen Weihs, artist*, will interact with a peer group and cultural organizations to further her knowledge of the artistic outside world; take yearly excursions to art museums, artist shows, and conventions. *Karen Weihs, artist*, will let her artist brain daily inspire and guide her, taking time to view the world, to touch objects of irregular shape and form, and to be sensitive to shadow and light. *Karen Weihs, artist*, will take time, whenever possible, to give of herself to her family and to others; to bring clarity into the daily routine of life, to focus on what is important in life and to exorcise fear and worry.

   b. <u>Clients</u>: *Karen Weihs, artist*, will maintain a high standard of work for her clients, and establish fair prices for the work produced. *Karen Weihs, artist*, will promote her work among her peers and within the larger community.

2. *Karen Weihs, artist* will support and uplift her only employee, herself, with love, humility and responsibility. *Karen Weihs, artist*, will provide a quiet, restful work space in an effort to inspire, nurture and produce good work.

All these goals, mission statements and mind bending attitudes sound like work, but it's worth it. It's easy to feel overwhelmed and impatient with the process, but a creative mind is never quiet. Train your artist brain to embrace the quiet as well as the chaos. In the quiet, you will perceive the true nature of your creative journey. In the chaos you will be energized to see it through.

I often compare my journey to that of a trip down a river on a white water raft. Sometimes the water is calm and I am floating under a serene sky. At other times, the water is rough and the current propels me beyond my control, and I have to learn how to use the power of the river to my advantage. To be prepared for the turbulent times, I must work hard in the calm to perfect my skills as an artist, so that I bring all of my talent to navigate the rapids. If I am lucky, there are moments when the challenge of the river equals the skill I possess to master it and we are one. Those are the moments for which I live and work.

Begin your journey. Embrace both the positive and negative feelings and memories that shape and direct it. Exorcise your fears and push off. This is your one chance to chart your own course. Choose well.

■

> *To see things as they are, the eyes must be open; to see things as other than they are, they must open wider; to see things better than they are, they must be open to the full.*
>
> Antonio Machado

SELF   HELP

From an early age, I knew I was different. I learned differently, expressed myself differently, and made choices differently. I was the survivor of a difficult family plagued by hardships.

I was a small child when I first sensed that my father was two people. By day, he was my Dad, but by night, he turned into someone else. It wasn't until I was nine that I realized that this other person was affected by alcohol. My escape from these nightly transformations was to surround myself with my own world of creativity. One of the things I loved to do was assemble intricate shapes with the extensive tile collection that I stole on my nightly jaunt to the local construction site. After dinner, I'd hop on my bike and go straight to the building lot where the boxes of tiles were stacked. Carefully, I'd sort through them, taking only the colors I needed to complete my elaborate pattern. I'd heard that a den of snakes lived behind the boxes, but I didn't care. Nothing could have stopped me. I was driven. Without realizing it, I was becoming an artist.

Creating things was my way of holding on to a normal life. I drew everything I saw or imagined. Once, when I was alone and bored, and couldn't think of anything to draw, I suddenly noticed the wallpaper in the dining room. The next thing my mother knew, I had picked up a pen and was drawing the wallpaper pattern all over the protective pad for the table. She didn't try to stop me. As a matter of fact, it's still there today.

What I have found, as I've grown older, is that the level of normalcy in one's life is what one creates. You can't change other people, but you can change who you are, and where you want to place yourself. The fact that I retreated into my own world of creativity taught me a lot about *self* at a very young age. Ironically, if my family life had been more ordinary, I might not have begun the journey of *self*-discovery so early.

At first, the process of *self*-discovery was painful, but now I welcome it. It gives me perspective on the realities of my life and makes me honor and value the path I have chosen. The only way to realize your creativity is to have faith in your *self*, trust yourself and love your *self*. In order to develop a strong sense of *self*, you have to set goals that lead to actions, emotions and choices that ultimately define who you are. Sometimes this can seem selfish, but it's really *self*-realized. The fruits of your focused, creative process will come back to those you love and the society you live in. And if your choices are wise and true to your *self*, your emotions will only be positive, with a sense of purpose, edging out the negative emotions.

Some people say to me in my classes things like: "I know what I want to do, but I can't make it happen!" or "I feel blocked!" For externally directed people, it is especially difficult to try to get in touch with *self*. Only when they are confronted with their own inner frustration do they learn internal direction. Creative people, by definition, are internally directed and constantly engaged in defining and confronting *self*. Negativity blocks that process, so the first exercise for the creative wanderer has already been perfectly captured in a song: "Accentuate the positive. Eliminate the negative, and so long to Mr. In-between." Apply that and your search for *self* will progress.

One particular friend of mine exemplifies this positive, passion driven definition of the creative soul. His name is Dr. Sewell Dixon, a well-known cardiovascular surgeon whose dream is now to unite scientific medicine with the powers of metaphysical healing to establish a health-enhancement center. To that end, he retired early and began to work on combining his knowledge of traditional health care with that of holistic-natural medicine — "the best of both worlds," he says.

When I asked him how his innovative concept was inspired by creativity, he responded with one word — "enrapture." For him, the entire process was passionate from the moment the idea came to him to the day-by-day realization of his dream.

How many well-established doctors would give up their lucrative practices to risk everything on such a controversial idea? The answer is — very few, but not because others haven't thought of it. The difference is passionate conviction, and that comes from believing in yourself more than in the skeptics who surround you.

One of Dr. Dixon's great gifts as a cardiac specialist is his intuition about patients and their particular conditions. Training and experience are great teachers, but some things cannot be taught. Dr. Dixon's intuitive approach to his patients' diagnoses and treatment is invariably correct, and yet he can't always point to a page in a medical book to explain why. He simply trusts his gift and uses it wisely in the unselfish service of others.

Dr. Dixon describes self as "needing to own your imagination and dreams." He freely admits that his *self* consisted of two distinctive parts — the one that worked and believed in the established health care system, and the other that recognized the need for alternatives outside the system. "The path to a successful venture," he added, "is very lonely, but worth the sacrifice to realize a passionate goal."

To me, his story illustrates the power and self-satisfaction of an independent life, fueled by the courage of creativity.

There have been times when I've lost my sense of *self*. Once, when I was just beginning to realize a level of success in my art, my youngest son decided to test my confidence by rebelling in every way a teenager will. For a long time, he won. He got my attention, but I lost all confidence as a mom and lost interest in my art. At times like that, you can't go it alone. Luckily there was an unusual group of mentoring parents at his school who led us back to a more stable life together. The unexpected, positive lesson from this experience was that I learned to "let go", and to let my son take responsibility for his own growing up. The way I did it was by concentrating on my own direction and letting him see me cope with success and failure. Gradually, he learned to take responsibility for the consequences of his successes and failures, and his first adult steps were taken.

Over the years I've learned a few things about the search for a creative *self*. You must be constantly nurtured and challenged with new ideas, thoughts and feelings. Surround yourself with the people, places and objects that give you energy and inspiration. Open up and share things that come naturally to you. Seek knowledge in everything that you do and you will enjoy a deeper awareness of your *self*. Be aware of the rich past of other creative people, so that you may put your own work into perspective. Acknowledge the part that luck plays in your own success, and don't be afraid of competition. Welcome serious cooperation in your field of work. The rewards of collaboration often surpass the achievements of any one individual. Enjoy the process of creating for its own sake. Learn by trial and error, and look for original ways to solve problems. It is through this technique known as "divergent thinking" that you will find your own unique creative solutions. Try not to mind too much what other people think. Nothing of worth comes without a price. Be your own best friend, not your own worst enemy.

Summon the courage to place your work in the public eye. Critical reaction, both positive and negative, will heighten your sensitivity and add another dimension to your sense of *self*.

Reviewers and bosses often wag their professional fingers at new ideas and original interpretations, unearthing childhood guilt. After all, your parents are your toughest critics for much of your developing life. The reviewer or boss simply steps into those shoes. If they are angry, disappointed, offended or threatened, they will berate you and try to make you feel ashamed of what you have done. To persevere, you must develop a skin thick enough to endure the "shaming" with all its past anger, and overcome it. The antidote for shame is *self*-love and *self*-praise.

The first time I was reviewed in print, it was great, but the second time, I was deeply hurt, and had to fight to rise above it. With the support of sympathetic friends, and the desire to prove the reviewer wrong, I got back to work.

Several months later, this critic had a show of her own. Exhibiting uncharacteristic self-control, I went up to her and congratulated her on her show and wished her continued success. As a parting shot, I thanked her for her devastating review of my work, informing her that "it had afforded me the opportunity to rise above her negativity and mature." It felt good leaving her with her mouth hanging open and nothing to say.

The single greatest deterrent to developing your creative *self* is fear. Fear of failure and humiliation. This old enemy, led by ego, is usually learned in our younger years and perpetuated by self-consciousness. No one wants to be embarrassed or appear the fool. When you create something, you open yourself up to criticism on the most personal level. It's frightening, but ultimately the risks you take will expand you, deepen you and enrich you.

It's your choice. Seek your creative *self*.

> *Artists must sacrifice to their art. Like bees, they must put their lives into their sting.*
> Emerson

42" x 56" oil on canvas

Take Two

Often to start an intuitive painting, I begin with compatible colors in a process called 'color blocking' on the canvas. Color blocking is the process of building a patchwork quilt of color and shape. When the patterns are established, I stand back to look at the painting as a whole. Usually at this stage an idea begins. In this painting the idea of film and movie related images began to form when looking at some of the shapes. I then begin to layer form, line and color on top of the background to introduce images into the whole of the painting. Abstractly, the painting works because of the shapes created by these color blocks. Expressionistically, it works because of the line, image, and texture imposed over it. While I am inventing the painting, I try to make it fun and satisfying to my own eyes. I play with all my materials, tools and techniques including wiping, sanding, splattering and layering. The desire and attitude to feel free, creatively free is essential. The rest is easy. I breathe life into my idea and let it come *Out of My Mind*. *Take Two* is owned by Tyson Weihs.

36" x 36" oil on canvas

The Diva

The Diva was a fun play of shapes and colors. I started with warm yellows and reds with my usual color blocks, dividing them into four uneven parts. These serve as a base for the finished color. My friend and peer, Dixie Dugan, calls these color blocks a play or puzzle from large to small shapes, calling them *Papa Bear, Mama Bear,* and *Baby Bear.* She always tells me, when I ask her to critique my work, if I have my family of shapes balanced or not. When I haven't succeeded in choreographing my fundamental shapes, I then play with them until they work. Shapes in abstract painting must vary in size or the painting is boring.

I often start thinking of color and figure shapes with no plan in mind, hoping the shapes in the painting will play off of each other directing me toward a plan. Here, the shapes seem to work strongly with the textures. The graceful body movement implied a figure which I invented. I realized there was a direction toward drama so I implemented fringe and feathers. The blue shapes on the upper right were shadows from my studio blinds. It broke up the green area and finished the painting. Sometimes accidents or shadows give clues toward what to do in a painting.

MIND MATTERS

Your ultimate goal as a creative person is to work "out of your mind" — out of your thinking mind.

The first time I worked "out of my mind" was in a design class in 1972 at the University of Georgia. The class was given the assignment to formulate a design for marketing purposes. I decided to design boxes for objects I found while exploring the Georgia countryside. The objects included shards, arrowpoints, barn artifacts, etc. For each object, I created its own container. Designing the container, the logo for the object, inventing its description, as well as writing the marketing script for the entire package taught me to trust my imagination, and not be afraid of my own ideas.

Eighteen years later, I have finally learned to trust myself again; eighteen years of different paths taken to build my confidence.

The important thing is to stretch your mind. Admit no limits. The journey is both fulfilling and frustrating, but requires maturity, time and patience to develop. I have come a long way from conventional calligraphy to painting large, abstract expressionistic canvases. Each step had to be taken, both forward and back for the journey to be mine. I chose painting, but others choose business, medicine, or a service industry to fulfill their creative predisposition. Whatever your choice or interest, you will be engaged in a push-pull direction, one step forward, two steps back, a leap forward, and then a pause to reflect. Each new thought, each new discovery of skills propel you to a heightened level of independence and expression. The only way I discovered painting was by trying things, failing, rising above the failure and starting again. Painting is now my job. I respect it. I value it. I celebrate it. I paint to sell, but I also paint for myself, for my own amazement. I enjoy the process of mastering skills, setting painting goals, and trusting my intuition.

All creative people struggle with their personal definition of creativity. Don't expect anyone to understand yours. What matters is that you define it for yourself and live by it.

My own personal definition is that it is a balance between the fruits of the spirit and the demons of the soul! Life is a struggle, especially if you expect the best from it. If you aspire to make something from nothing, you will suffer many failures. I have made many bad decisions on the way towards realizing a good painting, but I have also made enough good ones to keep me going. Sometimes you learn more from failure than success. One professor of mine critiqued my work by saying, "You have succeeded, indeed, but in failure." Puzzled, I asked, "Which part is the success and which part is the failure?".

"Do a few more and you'll find out," he said.

Years later, I learned the meaning of his comment. Every failure is a success, and without falling down, there is no getting up. Maya Angelou once said, "When you know better, you'll do better." Fall down, get up; fall down again and get up again. You should know better by this time, and you'll stop falling down. There is no right and wrong; only lessons to learn.

Basically, there are two characteristics of the creative personality: the **Conservative** and the **Expansive**. The "Conservative" is made up of conforming instincts for self-preservation while the " Expansive" is made up of instincts for exploring new things and taking risks. The curiosity necessary for creativity belongs to this latter half, but you need both, however. The "Conservative" requires little encouragement or support from the outside to motivate behavior while the "Expansive" can wilt if it is not cultivated. If too few opportunities for curiosity are available; if too many demands prevent the chance for risk taking and exploration, the motivation to engage in creative behavior is easily discouraged.

Everyone is creative, but are some more creative than others? Is a painter or writer more creative than a banker, attorney, or nurse? Not necessarily. Creative people usually possess an open and expansive view of the world; their *attitude* determines their choice to be creative. Their work is not proscribed. There are no legal guidelines, no rules and no parameters. Anything goes! We all develop a certain conservative or traditional approach to life, but creative people defy and transcend that approach to create their own expansive view of life.

A banker once visited my home to talk to me about doing a special commission for one of his new businesses.

"You are so creative," he said. "I wish I possessed this kind of creativity, but unfortunately, I am not at all creative."

I asked about his accomplishments as a banker, and he told me about his idea for banker implementing *Master Card* and *Visa* into the banking industry, which changed the banking industry as we know it.

"Don't you think that idea is creative?" I asked.

"Yeah," he said, "it was the most innovative implementation in my banking career."

"See—you're as creative as I am. You just don't know it. The only difference is your vision involves achieving goals in business instead of putting paint on canvas."

You must choose an original path to achieve your own creative goals. You must always embrace challenges and know your skills. When your creative skills merge with creative goals, anything is possible! You have the capability of making the world a more interesting and inspiring place to live — no matter what your profession.

Recently, I visited The Landing's Jazz on the River, a club in San Antonio's River Walk area, where the owner, Jim Cullum, plays the horn nightly with jazz greats whom he invites to play for his audience. His love of music, his creative approach to business, and the inspiration from his community of music lovers all combine to create this special experience for the visitor. Every night is new; each performance spontaneous—the essence of creativity.

Music artists, actor artists, and writer artists receive most of the attention for being creative, but bankers, painters, chefs, homemakers, landscapers, teachers, etc. work just as creatively. When I listen to live jazz, or read a spectacular novel, I wonder why some talented people get picked to rise above all the others. Luck and hard work! Educating yourself, working on yourself, and positioning yourself to be in the right place at the right time often determines the ones who will rise to the kind of fame we have come to know as "star power". In the art world, the museum curator, the gallery owner, and the art collector are the ones who choose a particular artist whose style in their opinion could change the art in our culture. The chosen ones are those who follow a unique path to their art form; a path that startles observers; a path that stirs up excitement, reaction and response. I know people all around me who fit that description. Unfortunately, they have missed the element of luck, which would have escalated them into "star power." Not all of us can be stars, as defined by the media, but we can possess an **attitude** of "star power." We can all rise to fame in our world, as we know it, by using this **attitude** of positive, self-directed goals. Your state of mind matters.

The four strengths one needs to be confident enough to succeed are: **attitude**, **intuition**, **goals** and **skill**. First, you need to develop a "yes I can" **attitude** about yourself which will enable you to trust and follow your creative **intuition**. Your **intuition** is the muse that inspires you.

It takes a long time to recognize it and listen to it, but, following your creative intuition will eventually help you realize your creative **goal**, which is the third strength. The fourth strength is creative **skill**. Knowing how to do something well completes the formula for realizing your creativity.

Attitude + Intuition + Goals + Skill = Success

To be successful and fulfilled in every facet of your life requires work. That is the four letter, all powerful word. Having a good creative attitude with an instinct for intuition is not enough. You must work at learning skills to help reach your goals. Education, exposure, experience, reasoning, common sense, and practice, practice, practice are necessary to master any skill. Not everyone is born with pure talent, and the ones who are, still have to work hard to complete their goals. Talent is 10%, while **attitude, intuition, skills** and clear **goals** make up the remaining 90%. If you are lucky enough to have a little talent, the formula $A + I + S + G = Success$ is enhanced by it, and becomes:

$A + I + S + G \times T = Success$

In my case and others, talent has come from the time spent mastering my skills. If you are a painter, paint every day. If you are a writer, write at least a little every day, and you will gradually elevate your skill level.

A perfect example of the success of this formula is the maverick criminal lawyer, Bill Diehl, a charming Charlotte, N. C. based raconteur described in North Carolina Business Magazine as "a small Incredible Hulk emerging as a junkyard dog." Bill realized his traditional lawyering success in spite of his rebellious nature. He says, "his greatest accomplishment has been surviving his badness, pushing the limits, breaking rules to create remarkable memories." He always works harder than his opponent, and his **goal** is to win through **attitude** and passion. The context of losing is an acceptable possibility, but the **goal** is to win. Objectively, the measure of a successful trial lawyer is the "win," but the **goal** is sometimes modified to embrace the "try."

Sporting his trademark long hair for the past 29 years, Bill comes across as a rumpled, quirky, skilled technician with a big heart who creatively outworks and outsmarts just about everybody. From defending Indian mystic Bhagwan Shree Rajneesh to pro wrestler Ric Flair; to Richard Dortch, the PTL's top ministry aid, Bill has made an effort not to look or act like other lawyers, while employing brilliant and surprising courtroom strategies to outwit his opponents. He admits to having been a mediocre student but gutsy. For him, creativity is being persistent in how you choose to live and behave. I would add to that the courage to follow through. Creative types are often misunderstood and viewed as confused, different, unpredictable and unreliable because of their individuality. Obviously, Bill Diehl has had the time of his life creatively balancing his behavior between risk and reward.

Success can be yours. Your state of mind matters.

In my own life, I've worked hard to apply the magic formula:

Attitude + Intuition + Goals + Skill = Success.

Once it all came together for me, when few doubted it could. In 1995, I helped found a full-time artists' co-operative gallery, The Waterfront Gallery, in Charleston, South Carolina. What is unusual about it is that it's owned and operated by its members, who are now juried in to exhibit.

When I got the idea to form a gallery in this unique space in the historic district of downtown Charleston, many were skeptical. With many artists crying — no money, no time, no energy, I argued that we had to ride the cultural wave of our city before greed consumed it.

Gradually, more began to share my vision as they saw opportunities slipping out of the hands of individual artists, and the cooperative concept was born. We sought like minds with diverse talents. Some knew business, some knew law and others knew marketing.

After many months of meetings and negotiations with our landlord, a star was born. With the sweat equity of our members' families and friends, who hammered and nailed and painted, we renovated our space. Attorneys, financial brains and marketing minds worked "pro-bono" to lead us through the technical mazes. Even our landlord, impressed with our passion and work, gave us a generous, long-term lease.

With every passing year, we have gained a little more fame and monetary success.

Who said artists and business don't mix?

Who said artists can't respect rules?

Who said artists can't work together towards a common goal?

Our success proves that **attitude**, **intuition**, **goals** and **skill** multiplied by a lot of talent equals success.

Your state of mind matters.

"Success is a journey not a destination — half the fun is getting there."
Gita Bellin

This piece was done for my son Justin's room. It was a piece designed for him, expressing his joy for life. It hung in his room for a long time before I decided to enter it in competition for the Spoleto, USA Festival poster for 1995. It won! Justin was very excited for me. Then, someone wanted to purchase it, and we decided to sell it, and split the money. Later, Justin told me he was sorry we had sold it, and he wanted it back. So I repainted it as best I could. The second version hangs in his room today. It is a painting expressing the joy of having a son like Justin. The dark suggests the challenge of raising an independent, free spirit, and the bright suggests the colorful side of parenting. Together, they express my feeling of being a parent. There is joy, there is angst, and there is always a glimmer of hope. Now that my daily parenting is almost done and my sons are soon to be adults, I can say the dance was not without stumbles, but it was, nevertheless, a perfect harmony of music, timing, and the appropriate steps.

44" x 52" oil on canvas

Musical Muse

This large painting started out as a vertical and ended up a horizontal. A figure appeared in the early stage of color blocking in cool, blue tones, then a shape similar to a guitar entered the painting from my imagination. I don't know why I started to paint a guitar shape, but, nevertheless, my hand always goes with what my mind and heart tells it to do. I started to wipe it out, but the wiping stroke was interesting and my intuitive muse voice said, "Leave it!". I then turned the painting on the horizontal and I started to brush into the shapes with yellow, its complement. It flowed from left to right in a pattern suggesting a figurative shape in motion. I played upon it and finished the painting when I thought the motion was effectively captured. Beth and Jim Stuckey own this painting.

A Positive
State of the Art

The best way to become more positive is to do what you know how to do well, then act as if you know how to do the rest. Gradually, the rest will get easier, and your fear of not being able to accomplish what you've set out to do will lessen.

Every time I sit in front of my easel, I am afraid. I fear that I won't be able to pull off the next painting; that I'm not good enough. Fear is a daily demon which creeps into all of our lives. My solution to fear is to welcome it, invite it in, entertain it, challenge it, and then send it away. Having a negative self-image is not productive. The way to get up the courage to work in spite of fear is to affirm yourself and what you're doing. Remind yourself every day what you believe. Read your mission statement each morning and keep adding to your creative credo. Two motivating thoughts from which I draw particular strength and energy are written on top of my easel: "I embrace life!" and "If you believe it, you can do it!"

After all these years, I can honestly say that my biggest fear is not doing what gives me joy. Georgia O'Keefe once said, "I've been terrified all my life, but that hasn't stopped me from doing the things I've wanted to do."

That was not always true for me. At one time in my life, when I least believed in myself, a man named Frank did. He became my mentor and through him, I developed a sense of confidence. You've heard the phrase, "When the pupil is ready, the master will appear." Frank Licciardi was my master.

Frank and his wife appeared in my life years ago when my children were preschoolers. My boys and my freelance graphic design business consumed my days. My husband was busy developing and running restaurants. Frank was an established Midwest artist who moved to Charleston for health reasons. Luckily, he rooted near me. We all quickly became friends. Soon, he invited me to watch him paint and have coffee with him and his wife a couple of mornings a week while my boys were in nursery school. I never aspired to be a professional artist except in my dreams, but Frank convinced me of my creative potential, and I began to listen.

His positive attitude, love of life, and immense skill and intuition inspired me daily. He was prolific in spite of his health problems. After a while, a few of us gathered to draw and paint with Frank on a regular basis. His wife, always so jolly, served us coffee and laughed with us like a sister. It was then that I began clearing the first hurdles of learning an artist's skills, acquiring an artist's attitude, setting goals and acknowledging inspiration as the path to creativity. It's Frank's formula that I recommended to you and now live by:

Attitude plus Intuition combined with Goals and Skills equal Success.

Frank received his classical training at the Chicago Art Institute and the American Academy of Art. He had painted from an early age, always selling his art, but did not decide to become a full time artist until he was fifty-seven. He really learned to paint on his own while running several classy bars and raising nine children. After the children were older, he gave up his other businesses and concentrated totally on his art. He was humble, and ever so proud at the same time. He didn't drink, and he was proud of it. He gained power through pain, and he acquired love by showing love. He painted from his mind, and, literally, out of his mind. But he also painted from reality, making insightful portraits with unbelievable character.

During the times when the fear factor would hit me pretty bad, Frank would shelter me with kind words and careful teaching. Each day, I would arrive with an idea for a painting, and he would listen first and then challenge me with questions. There was always a give and take with mutual respect. Just watching him work day in and day out, through trial and error, was enough of a visual lesson to teach me about the physical discipline of creative endeavor.

Frank only had one leg, having lost the other to lyomyosarcoma, a rare malignancy of the walls of the arteries. He had survived a heart attack, quadruple by-pass surgery and two strokes. He lived only ten years after I met him, and he was the single most important person in the awakening of my creative and productive life.

Another person, who has helped me to believe in myself and the human spirit is my sister, Lynn, a wonderful woman who just happens to have cerebral palsy. Lynn has accomplished more than some healthy people accomplish in their lifetime. Learning to walk artificially at age eight; learning how to speak with a permanent impediment, to more recently, surviving a near fatal automobile accident and coming back to her normal life, she has always been an inspiration to me. If she can run a business, write two books with three more in their planning stages, then any of us can change our **attitude**, develop strength and **intuition**, learn a **skill**, and set **goals** for ourselves.

The power of talk among friends is another source of support and affirmation. I call it "magic talk." Many times I have felt overwhelmed by juggling my roles as a daughter, wife, mother, friend, businessperson, teacher and artist. My soulmate friends give me the freedom and courage to grow through the power of words and sharing. Someone said to me once, "If something overwhelms you, put it (even if it's <u>you</u>) into an imaginary box; store it away in your mind, and bring it out when you are ready to deal with it!"

I find that my friends allow me to bring out the box, open it up, face the problem unafraid and handle it. They affirm my soul and give me the energy to climb, crawl or leap out of the box myself. I am now fond of leaping out of boxes.

Recently, I entertained my best friend from childhood and my best friend as a grown up for a girls' weekend. Both are dear to me and our magic talk brought out a new dimension in all our lives.

Sherry has been a friend since I was 13 and Paula for the last fifteen years. Sherry was my opposite, a big achiever, winning many scholarships, working very hard in spite of financial worries. I was distracted, an average student who never worried about money (even though there was never enough) and graduated by the seat of my pants. Sherry kept me focused and reaffirmed me daily. Although we were different, we shared the same passion and perseverance for our creative goals. Ironically, we both married young, and sacrificed our creative ambitions temporarily to insure financial security.

Money is a necessary evil in an artist's life. Adequate income is required to live. Extra income is required to free more time for creative pursuits. The ideal is the union of creative work with monetary reward. Most artists spend their lives balancing the two. Sherry and I are not the exception.

Sherry became a devoted 7th grade teacher who uses the classroom as a stage for her creative talents. Her talents are logic, personality, humor, and soul goodness. In my mind, she could have been the female Bill Gates or the first woman president. In her mind, I was always an artist with an **A**ttitude. We have surprised each other with our successes, and reaffirmed each other by our loyalty through the years.

Paula, a nurse whose creativity is "joie de vivre," pointed out that I did it the unconventional way, and Sherry did it the conventional way, yet we are all now creatively pursuing our goals. It's wonderful when new and old friends accept the good and the bad in you and reaffirm who you are.

When I met Paula, it was like finding the ideal prom dress at my favorite boutique, a perfect fit, diminishing my flaws. She came to one of my classes, kept us all laughing, was an intermittent student, but nonetheless a creative one. The next time I saw her was at a party. She locked us inside the bathroom for nearly an hour to gossip. We are like Thelma and Louise who have been asked to serve punch at The Cotillion (which we have spiked of course) and are just waiting for the opportunity to sneak away and jump on the Harleys that are revved up out back for us. Her creative talents are surfacing during mid-life.

Although many of us have friends and peers who affirm us, some of us are lucky enough to have creative soul partners. All of my married life, my husband and I have pitched in to support each other's career whenever needed.

When I met Chris in 1971, I was a student, and he had come to this country in 1969 from his native Germany — a young man with an energetic work ethic, unpolished English with six hundred dollars in his pocket. He still is the same productive, creative man he was then, and quite irresistible. During our courtship, he kept surprising me with intricately planned dates like visiting a remote island to photograph ibis or sampling bistros for the perfect dessert. Always with flowers and complements. Eventually, he swept me off my feet, and we were married.

We started out with a little money and a lot of hard work, but, together, we developed a "bounce" effect partnership, which meant that whoever came up with an idea, the other would give it full support.

When Chris wanted to quit the world of Hyatt and Marriott, after climbing the corporate ladder, he knew that he would be risking everything on his dream of becoming an independent restauranteur. We took that risk together, and Chris did more than realize his dream. In 1997, he sold the last of his seven restaurants for top dollar.

Working together in an equal partnership keeps our energy high and we are constantly learning from each other. Chris has worked hard to understand my artist brain, and my need for independent, creative time, while I have learned the importance of organization and timing from his restaurant business. Both of us have developed our creative selves by affirming each other.

Accentuate the positive.

Be grateful.

Affirm your creative self.

Celebrate the creative process with others.

Find your soul mate.

30" x 30" oil on canvas

Self Portrait

After Frank died, I painted *Self Portrait*. Once again, a hand other than mine guided me. It finished itself. A spiritual sense of trust and conscience took over the intuitive production of this painting. I call this Self Portrait because, as I look upon this painting, which seems so foreign to me, I realize once again another form of consciousness compelled me to look at myself from this perspective. This is an impression of my body in my youth, somewhat disjointed and awkward. The balls that are being juggled in the painting symbolize the forces which controlled my life and consciousness for so many years; a home with an alcoholic parent, another parent feeling overwhelmed, a strong-willed sibling born with, what could have been, a very debilitating physical handicap. The balls represent the part of my 'soul', which shielded itself remarkably from those forces when it needed to be protected. They are finally released into the air and I am free of them. It is this same 'soul', which made me paint this painting, that is putting these words together for me. The painting reassures me that those three dark shadows behind me are shrouded and drifting away. Their gloomy hold on me is weakening.

> *The last human freedom is to choose your attitude no matter what the circumstances.*
>
> Victor Frankle,
> *Holocaust survivor*

The juggling act, which I did so well for so many years, is separate from my body now. There is love there, fringed with the mystery of life. What is in the past is history, and it is this mystery that makes me what I am today. It was a force, which became my destiny. Love with family comes in a new way, in a healing that is beyond my control, and I welcome it!

The landscape in the background is clear, and nature, which has been my retreat, is light and vast, with more growth springing up in the distance. There is separation between me and the shadowed people. The bright window is my escape and future promise. I stand emotionally strong and free of guilt. I know that the people who have entered my life now are there for a reason. They are gifts. Some are family, some are spiritual friends, while others are soul mates and artistic compatriots. Each time I put my brush to canvas, I find a new clue to what my life means — beyond the every day surfaces of life. I am learning to relinquish power to intuitive consciousness. I only know that letting myself paint beyond my control is a gift I must accept and pursue without fear.

36" x 36' oil on canvas

I Hear Music Playing

Often, I start a painting with nothing in mind but color blocking. Choosing a muted green palette with complementary warm red tones, I put on my favorite music, which is beach, boogie and blues music. This is popular on the East Coast. Hoping the music will inspire me this time, I start thinking about being young on the beach with friends.

I lost a friend in a tragic accident when we were nineteen. He loved to dance the shag, and loved beach music. Soul music strengthens me when I think of his lost youth. The past can't be changed, but energy can be drawn from it, and this painting captures the exuberance and emotional pain I feel from that time and that loss.

I also think of my artist friend, Frank Licciardi — my mentor, whom I mentioned earlier in the book, who taught me to use music while painting. Before his death from cancer at 75, he taught me enough about being an artist to last me a lifetime. He also taught me about friendship. When we painted together we always listened to music; orchestral, opera, and Bing Crosby being Frank's favorites. (I could never get him to love beach music.) When I was working on this painting, Frank's strength came back to me, as it often does.

30" x 40' oil on canvas

Here's Looking At You

Here's a painting I did for an eye wear boutique, for the owners of the boutique, who are friends and an inspiration to me. They are creative, energetic, excited and open to life. Their energy, coupled with mine, sparked an insight into this painting. The painting began first with an area of color, followed by an interesting color pattern. After I liked the pattern of color and the rhythm of shapes, I started seeing how I could intimate the idea here and there to suggest people's shapes with eye wear shapes. For a while, the creative process took over and I lost my sense of time and space. Only then did I realize that this was definitely going to be the boutique's painting. I didn't think this was their painting until I got into it, and it turned out to be funky, fun, and colorful, just like the boutique and its owners, Jack and Beth Schaeffer.

TRAITS RATE

Creative people share certain paradoxical traits which have been documented by Mihaly Csikszentmihaly in his book, *Creativity.*

Before I read his book, I knew that there were conflicting aspects to my personality, but I never attempted to understand them. Raised traditionally, I learned to walk the conventional path, while always leaning a bit toward the unconventional. My personality was both introverted and extroverted. I felt instinctively creative, but underplayed it, because of the critical view of those around me. I was self-conscious, as most of us are until we're about 45 and figure it all out.

Years later, I was to learn these paradoxical characteristics and personality traits were natural to creative people.

1. Energetic yet quiet and calm
2. Smart yet naïve
3. Playful yet disciplined
4. Imaginative yet rooted in reality
5. Extroverted and introverted
6. Humble yet proud
7. Masculine and feminine
8. Conventional yet rebellious
9. Passionate yet objective
10. Anguished yet joyous

Consider each set of dual traits and how they apply to you.

1. Energetic yet quiet and calm. Creative people can work long hours while remaining fresh and enthusiastic. They can focus like a laser beam, but often take rests and sleep a lot. They are energetic but not hyperactive. They tend to learn by trial and error.

Today, some of those same people are diagnosed with Attention Deficit Disorder (ADD). My youngest son and I were diagnosed with ADD, and we both identify with this first trait. The test results for this disorder suggest that these people learn by trial and error rather

33

> *"I learn by going where I have to go."*
> T. Rothke

than by rote. We have a lot to learn about alternative ways of teaching children who cannot learn by memorization and formulas. I was intimidated by traditional testing methods. I learned best by experimentation, writing, discussion, and writing. As an artist, I learned to paint and design by imitation. You show me, I'll do it. Experimentation and spontaneity proved to be my method of getting things done.

2. Smart yet naïve. Creative people are smart and intuitive with a spontaneous, pure, sometimes child-like view of the world. They are driven to create, and enjoy a certain innocence or naivete in the face of reality. Their naivete protects them from becoming cynical and ceasing to find purpose in their work. It is why creative people marvel at the shape of a sea shell or tremble at the sound of a cello. Because of their naivete, they rarely become jaded, and never lose their sense of wonder.

> *The real act of discovery consists not in finding new lands, but in seeing with new eyes.*
> Marcel Proust

3. Playful yet disciplined. These duel traits are sometimes described as responsible and irresponsible. When I'm feeling playful, I am easily distracted and discover new interpretations in my work. Both traits are important — the former for spontaneity, the latter for results. When disciplined, I achieve goals. The challenge is in balancing the need to focus and my desire to play and experiment in myriad directions. The outcome keeps me laughing at myself.

> *"Two things are required: a brain and the willingness to spend long hours thinking, with a definite possibility that you come out with nothing."*
> Hans Bethe

4. Imaginative yet rooted in reality. I am a realist. I live a traditional life, but I inject imagination into its routine frequently. I always try to instill a sense of adventure in my children, especially when faced with the more mundane daily chores of life. Imagination played a large part in my childhood and in the rearing of my own children. As an artist, it is the only way I work. I plunge into my imagination searching for images to express my feelings.

> *Imagination is the beginning of creation. You imagine what you desire; and at last you create what you will."*
> George Bernard Shaw

5. Extroverted yet introverted. Both are stable traits that differentiate people, but creative individuals express both traits. I was an introverted observer of the world as a child. I still like the aloneness of painting, but now my extroverted adult personality enjoys the camaraderie of others, especially other creative people. I gain inspiration from others. The business world, in which my husband participated, provided so much social contact that painting was a necessary escape. I need the social stimulation as well as the solitude to create.

> *"In solitude, we give passionate attention to our lives, to our memories, to the details around us."*
> Virginia Wolfe

6. Humble yet proud. Often creative people are shy and self-deprecating when one expects arrogance and hubris. Pride is taken in the work, but public response is humbling, and the slightest compliment can be disconcerting. Sometimes, I feel overwhelmed by people, especially groups of people reacting to my work, and yet I want to show my work and need to hear people's reactions to it.

7. Masculine and feminine. Psychological androgyny is not sexual but refers to a person's ability to be both aggressive and nurturing, sensitive and rigid, dominant and submissive, regardless of gender. Men major in masculinity and minor in femininity while women major in femininity and minor in masculinity. Strength and sensitivity are both essential aspects of the creative spirit. You have to be both tender and tough to persevere as an artist.

8. Conventional yet Rebellious. You need to learn the conventional rules of your chosen discipline before you can effectively rebel against them. You must know what has come before in order to launch into a new direction. Respect the knowledge and skills of the past, and dare to do something different. You must understand the old myths in order to transcend them, and create new ones.

As an artist today, I break all the rules in painting, but I firmly believe you have to know the rules before you can successfully break them.

When I was a teenager, I insisted on a kooky wardrobe for parties, but loved traditional dressing for church. I designed and sewed my own clothes because the shops in my small town offered so little. I had fun developing my schizophrenic style and at one time, I thought I would become a fashion designer.

Georgia O'Keefe used to paint in the nude, the physical act of shedding social convention. Each of us has a wild streak that we must learn to tame and let loose when the creative spirit calls.

9. Passionate yet objective. Without passion, you'll soon lose interest in a difficult task, and yet without objectivity, your work suffers. After inspiration, your passionate side drives your work, while your objectivity keeps you on track. In other words, feel the passion but discipline the work.

10. Anguished yet joyous. This trait describes how the openness and sensitivity of creative individuals

"An artist is a person who takes uncommon responsibility for what he does."
Jonathan Benthall

"Living is a form of not being sure, not knowing what's next or how ... the artist never entirely knows. We guess. We may be wrong, but we take leap after leap in the dark."
Agnes de Mille

"Creativity is harnessing universality and making it flow through your eyes."
Peter Koestenbaum

It took me all my life to learn to paint as a child.
Piccasso

"What doesn't kill me makes me stronger."
Albert Camus

often expose them to as much suffering and pain as joy. The greater one's sensitivity, the more painful the slights. The greater the empathy, the deeper the anguish at the suffering of others. Likewise, the greater one's sense of joy in life, as well.

I know when I'm working at the top level of my own creativity, my cares and worries melt away and I experience a sense of bliss. The process is so rewarding that sometimes I am unable to part with the painting. Whatever pain or joy I have known in my life are both celebrated in my work.

In sharing the concept of these traits with one of my creative friends, Margaret summed it up perfectly in terms of her own work as a corporate consultant for improving the productivity of the work place.

"I did not know I was creative until I learned to take calculated risks and enjoy the result. When analyzing different levels of workers in a corporation, I had to be both attached and detached so I could be more creative. Sometimes my passion would get in the way. To help an organization really flourish, I had to step back and use my outside pair of eyes to be objective. Ultimately, I realized that I did not have all the answers because there were a multitude of ways to solve a problem. I learned to use mentors, to manage from my heart. I had to be serious minded and willing to take chances. This way of problem solving was sometimes difficult and painful, but now I enjoy this creative process that really is helping to make a better world through a better work place."

Congressman Mark Sanford of South Carolina is another person who exercises the many dual facets of his personality in a field where criticism and hypocrisy abounds. He is a quiet family man who believes deeply in public service. He exhibits a strong work ethic, but values equally the time spent with his children and his local community. He has sacrificed his private life to be a public servant. In politics, there are many great minds and ideals, but without the soul and the spirit behind them, they're wasted. Mark has both, and doesn't mind sacrificing his own comfort to get his message across. He spent many months sleeping in his office in Washington to save the taxpayers' money rather than rent a house or apartment. His passion has brought a young and enthusiastic energy and conscience to the congressional floor. He believes that human beings are more alike than different from each other, and he abjures the politics of division. His approach is tender yet tough; passionate yet objective.

If you feel these parallels in your personality, take comfort in being a complex, sometimes conflicting, individual. Don't be afraid of it. It is the driving force behind your creativity and the essence of your soul.

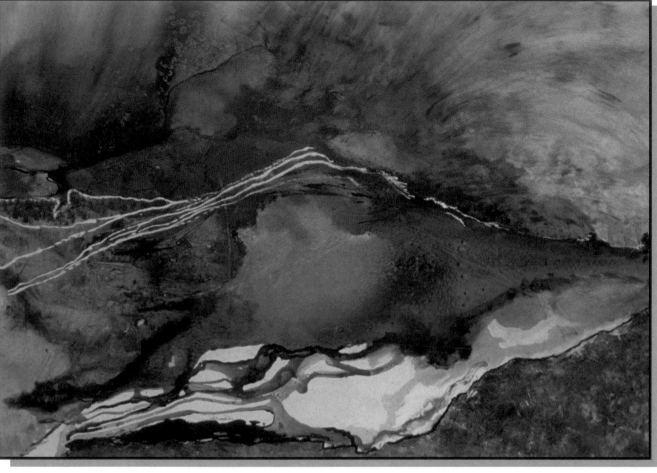

    This poured acrylic painting was definitely predetermined, an omen, a happening, a remembrance of time and events, all at once. My best friend, Paula, asked me to do a painting for her home, but she wanted to be a part of its creation. I went to her home in 1989 with paint, paper, and ready to have fun. We set up the room where it was to hang to gain inspiration from Paula's great taste in decorating. She told me, "Do it wild and woolly!" which definitely reflects her personality. While we were working, pouring paint, and discussing colors, and watching the paint take shape into something, we listened to the radio. Suddenly the announcer informed us that Hurricane Hugo would hit near Charleston in 24 to 30 hours. We poured, painted, and worried. We talked about making plans in case it hit us. "It will be bad!" the announcer went on to say, " because it will hit at high tide." We got a little panicked and looked down at the unfinished painting and we both said together, "It looks like a storm on paper!" "Eerie!" "Let's get out of here!" So away we went to prepare for the storm!

    It hit, and hit hard. We all went inland to escape it, since Charleston's Mayor Riley made evacuation mandatory.

Weeks later, with the hurricane behind us, I took out the painting and decided it should not be finished, since it was an omen and a special time shared with a friend. I only added a touch of gold and silver before framing it to express the gleam of hope in its conclusion. It hangs in Paula's home today as a reminder of the truth of intuition. When Paula's home is on Charleston's historical home tour, the painting gets the special story.

PAIN IN THE ART

Being creative is not easy.

It takes time, effort, concentration and commitment. Sometimes it even hurts.

Often it involves working hard at something that others don't at first appreciate or understand. It's easy to become discouraged or frustrated and give up, but there are ways to help you keep your creativity focused and thriving.

Are you exhausted by too many demands? Do you find yourself easily distracted? Do you not know what to do with your energy? Creating something out of nothing requires the right attitude conducive to spiritual growth. Here are some practical tools for realizing a more creative and spiritual life that artists have used for years.

1. Journaling

2. Explorative Time

3. Ridding yourself of the ones who make you crazy

4. Paying attention to detail

5. Active Listening

6. Visualizing

7. Completing the Task

8. Practicing awareness

9. Increasing complexity and challenge

1. JOURNALING can be done in the mornings, in the evenings, or when you're on the go, but it must be done religiously. It will require an effort on your part, but it is the primary tool for stimulating a creative attitude. A page per day is enough. If your start is slow, then begin with a few sentences, a paragraph, then build up to a page. Through journaling you will find your strengths and your personal demons. Without it, you will not be able to get in touch with your creative, artistic brain. Your artistic brain is sensitive to the sensual world around it, and causes deep "feeling"

responses to it. The creative brain is associative and subtle in its interpretations. Things are not viewed as simply black or white, but in shades of richly varied grays-misty, dusky, ashen, drab. The creative brain is freer in its associations, weaving together images and thoughts to invent new meaning about what is observed and experienced.

2. The second tool, EXPLORATIVE TIME, is a block of time set aside to nurture your creative consciousness, your inner self, the child within. It may be only two hours, but it is for you and you alone. It could be a play day or an excursion just for yourself. It need not cost any money. Go for a walk on the beach; hike up a mountain; wander into a junk store where you might find remembrances from your youth; visit a museum, or an old friend, or simply go to the movies, but devote this time to yourself.

3. The third tool is to RID YOURSELF OF THE ONE(S) WHO MAKE YOU CRAZY. They are the people who break deals and destroy your precious schedules. They are the ones who expect special treatment, discount your time, and cause discord, and disrupt your relationships. They are the ones who spend your time and money. They are the expert blamers. They hate order and they deny that they are crazy makers. They have their own agenda, and you will never own it. They use control dramas, interrogation tactics, aloofness, "poor me complaints" and intimidation. They think if they have control over you, they must be in control of themselves. If you are involved with crazy makers, get rid of them now! Otherwise, they will exploit you and block your creative flow. Ask yourself why you are involved with that type of person. Confront the reason. Resist it. Like a bad habit, you will eventually be able to give those crazies up.

Ironically, two of the people who have nurtured me the most are the same ones who can sometimes make me a little crazy. Although I love them very much, I must protect my creative side from their obsession with my time. I must separate their agenda from mine, put it away somewhere in the back of my mind, and carry on with my job as an artist. I cannot eliminate the people I love, but I can evaluate their demands on my life and deal with them carefully. I have learned not to drop everything I am doing to take on someone else's personal agenda. My job has become one of weighing conflicting demands on my time and acting accordingly. I have eliminated car pool crazy makers, committee delegators, and volunteer vampires! I have learned to say a kindly "No!" It takes a bit of give and take to achieve the balance that's right for you, but you're worth it!

4. The fourth tool is PAYING ATTENTION TO DETAILS. Train yourself to really look and experience the world around you. Look at the way light shines through a window, a palm tree sways, or shadows change color as the sun sets. Recognize the beauty in architecture, in the curve of a wave, in children humming, even in decaying, old walls. Listen to the words that people say or don't say. Watch their expressions, and their body language. Pay attention to the little things and a great deal more will be revealed.

5. The fifth tool is to become an ACTIVE LISTENER. Listening allows you to learn, to be stimulated and, ultimately, to be motivated to think creatively. Listening enriches your own thoughts. Someone else's idea may be the catalyst for a new idea of your own. You may even find a kindred spirit in someone you least expected, just because you listened and heard them.

6. COMPLETION OF THE TASK is the sixth tool. If you start it, finish it! Establish a time frame for completion and make it a learned behavior. It will free you to do more, and will help you to form good habits.

7. VISUALIZE who you want to be and what you want to accomplish. As a painter, I may visualize a scene or a feeling I want to paint. It may be an abstract or figurative painting, but the impetus is visualizing it first. At other times, I visualize myself standing at an easel and the inspiration to paint follows. Just like in the movie, *Field of Dreams*, if you build it, they will come. If you can visualize it, you can realize it. Remember, to be creative, it is your job to do the work, not to judge the work. You will have to paint a lot of bad paintings, write a lot of poor manuscripts, and discard a lot of ad campaigns before you succeed. The point is to keep doing the work.

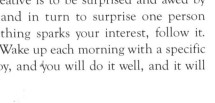

Visualizing has helped me as much as my painting. When I have to give a lecture, I visualize myself standing in front of all the people and enjoying the speech. When I remember the shy, naive girl who feared exposure to people, I realize how far I have come and take pride in my accomplishments and in my own growth!

8. PRACTICE AWARENESS. Other things you can do to make your life more creative is to be surprised and awed by something every day, and in turn to surprise one person each day. When something sparks your interest, follow it. Learn something new. Wake up each morning with a specific goal. Do what you enjoy, and you will do it well, and it will

reward you. Surprise yourself by trying something you think you can't do. Each time you do it, you will get better at it. Make time for relaxation and reflection. Plan your time and shape your space. Find out what you like and what you hate about life, and do more of what you like and less of what you hate.

9. Increase the COMPLEXITY of what you are doing, and you will never be bored. Learn to concentrate. If you focus your attention on what interests you, you will begin to aim for complexity. Through these practices, you will gain a sense of power as a highly creative individual. Establish and realize goals which will then create a body of experiences, emotions and choices that comprise your recognizable self. By setting new and more complex goals, the experience varies and remains interesting and a challenge. Like a weight lifter, with each increase of weight and challenge, the stronger and more skillful you become.

As a creative person, you must acknowledge all of your feelings and grow from them. Some people will try to make you feel guilty about your gifts and strengths. Never abandon yourself just to make others feel comfortable or good about themselves. You must come first, because you have special gifts, which need attention daily. I'm not telling you to abandon your loved ones, but only through an honest assessment of yourself will you begin to believe in your creative self. Share this knowledge with others and eventually they will understand, and recognize your talents.

Everyone is creative, but not everyone understands creativity (even when people possess it), so creative people are made to feel "different". If people work at understanding their own creativity, they become more secure in themselves and are able to understand and accept others. The only person you can change is yourself. Pursue your own creative path and you will inspire others to pursue theirs.

■

"Better to have a pain in the art than no pain(t) at all."

Karen Weihs

MIS EN PLACE

Before I start my day, I go through a process I call *mis en place*, which is French for "everything in its place," or, as I put it: **Get organized, both physically and mentally**. Through the external process of getting organized, I can internally organize myself. My husband's attention to *mis en place* taught me its value. In chef apprentice school, he was trained to put everything he needed in place before him so the job would be easy. Over the years, I have learned to do the same with my art.

Just like following a recipe when cooking a meal, I follow my own recipe of organization. I start with my list of organized time for that particular day. A calendar or a day timer works for most people. For me, it is my daily list that I rely on. Usually, the list is made the night before, then revised in the morning. It starts with telephone calls, things I need to buy, and business chores to do that day. The list also tells me how and when to organize my paint supplies as well as the studio clean up. Once I have completed the task of writing letters, applying to shows, and ordering supplies and frames, I can happily paint and feel good. Likewise in my home, a sense of *mis en place* is essential for harmony and balance. After my work as an artist is finished for the day, I tackle more personal issues, and only when that is put behind me can I make a list for the next day's work adventure, and enjoy a peaceful evening with my husband.

My routine of *mis en place* has varied at different times in my life. As a single person, and then as a young mother, I worked at night, and was rarely organized. Consequently, I frustrated myself. As my children grew, my organizational skills increased and I learned how to be more efficient. My production work then changed to mornings. Now, with my children living away, I organize in the mornings and produce in the afternoons. I'm sure this will change again as my life evolves.

Here is an example of why *mis en place* is so necessary. During the time that I was a freelance designer, I had young children so I worked at night on design commissions. Once I was given a job to design two wedding invitations for twin girls. They wanted different visuals, but the designs were very similar. Carefully I placed each set of designs in a separate pile on my studio desk, but my cat decided to sleep on the studio desk that night and scattered the visuals. Upon reorganizing the piles, I mixed up the instruction sheets, and the jobs were reversed. When the girls came to pick up the finished work, we were all horrified. I nearly collapsed working extra nights to correct the mistake and make the deadline. It was a hard way to learn about the importance of *mis en place*, but I never forgot it.

I'm not inspired to paint every single day, neither am I neurotically driven to produce for the sake of production. When I am having a session which is not turning into a productive paint day, I don't sweat it. I just go about the day organizing and preparing, filing, cleaning, or looking at art books. Sometimes I need to mentally separate myself from the tasks for a while and visit or shop with friends. The more I have organized during that time, the more time I will have when I am inspired to paint. Many times, ideas churn in my head while I'm organizing my studio. Time is not wasted with *mis en place*; it is part of the necessary process of creativity. That process includes the following stages:

⋯ **Preparation:** Preparation is when you are immersed enough in a subject to be curious about it.

⋯ **Incubation:** Incubation is the period of time when ideas churn around, just below the threshold of consciousness. Sometimes they surface in dreams, when driving a long distance, or during a hot bath.

⋯ **Insight:** Insight is the moment when all of the puzzle pieces come together to give you the excitement, or the "A-ha" of decision.

⋯ **Evaluation:** Evaluation is the stage where you step back and you ask yourself, "Is the endeavor worth doing?"

⋯ **Elaboration:** Elaboration is the actual permission you give yourself to do the work. This is when the 10% inspiration merges with the 90% perspiration. When the project is completed, there is no better "high" of achievement. It is this link of imagination and reality, which gives you the greatest sense of individual freedom.

This pyramid illustrates my division of time. *Production* (green) is the creative time. *Maintenance* (red) is the organization of things, (errands, home, home office, and personal belongings). *Leisure* (blue) is fun time, time spent involved with sports, friends, and children. This chart represents how our time should be divided. Without leisure time, maintenance time could be resented. Without production, we could not feed our souls and channel our creativity. We need equal doses to produce satisfactory goals.

The challenge to *mis en place* is the balance between the demanding life of children and family and the reclusive creative life. Prioritizing is therefore critical to *mis en place*. Knowing that I have an active and slippery mind makes me appreciate the need to organize and prioritize.

To apply *mis en place* in your life, you have to respect yourself and your work enough to set time, energy and space aside for it. For years I drove myself crazy by constantly criticizing every aspect of my role as artist, mom and wife. Now I am discovering that I have a choice about how I see myself and my life and how I feel about things. The more positive choices I make, the more love flows freely into my relationships with my husband, children and friends. Now I understand that self and self-love is about honoring oneself, and in turn, others. The process doesn't work in an orderly fashion, but if you use the self-love concept, the duties of work, marriage and family become more deep and personally satisfying. The object is not to be dependent on those whom you are emotionally attached to, but inter-dependent as a separate and secure individual.

Just recently I spent a night with my friend Paula and her children at their beach home on a small South Carolina barrier island. My husband was away for a month and my children were living away for the summer. It was my first empty nest experience. That night the moon was full, and my bed overlooked three large windows that gave on to the Atlantic Ocean where the moon shimmered on the ocean and I could hear the rustle of the swaying sea oats. I kept waking up. I didn't want to miss the smell and song of the surf. When you are at peace, alone, your thoughts become clear and your heart becomes ready for the next passage of life. *Mis en place* helps to foster those moments when place and circumstance inspire you.

Attitude has an effect on one's organizational skills as well. The "yes I can do it" attitude reinforces every creative decision. When I sit and organize my thoughts on how I wish to work, I make five commitments of intent.

1. I will respect my creative journey.
2. I will work with attitude.
3. I will be confident and secure in the creative process.
4. I will continue under all circumstances.
5. I will follow what I love and let it take me where it will.

Attitude is what makes art original and bold. Tight, detailed paintings are beautiful but laborious. They require infinite skill, but

45

lack emotional content. The hand of the artist is not felt except as a technical tool. There is no soul. "That looks just like a photo," is often the measurement for a successful work of art. That way of measuring art is how most artists first learn to work. Painting tight is easy and safe, and unimaginative.

The worse thing an artist can do is to be tempted to repeat him/herself. Just because the flower painting worked well last week isn't a good enough reason to reinvent it again the following week. The first painting was done in the spirit of the moment with everything working together to create a painting worthy of its time. To reinvent it will never work in the same manner. The spirit of doing fresh work has the edge on creativity. Loosen up. Finding your own style and expression can be frustrating and frightening, but it's worth it. Don't give up. Create with "attitude."

The desire to paint usually comes from a strong sense that all things are somehow connected—moving in a particular direction and bonded by some architecture of immense beauty. That is why I want to paint — to reach beyond the subject and tap into the power that moves behind it. Look at the work of artists who dare to create with *attitude* and you will begin to unlock the mystery of your own creative adventure.

A philosopher of music once said " The beauty of music lies not only in the notes, but also in the spaces between the notes. The silences enhance the sound by creating a mystery for the listener to interpret."

It occurs to me that this is true for artists, scientists, poets, and entrepreneurs. The silence in music is the equivalent of leaving something unfinished but open to interpretation by the one who experiences it. To get a mood, a feeling or a spirit in a painting requires more trust in your self, and the courage to experiment with technique.

Freedom is the link between imagination and reality.

I know it has been the "*accidents,*" which have taught me more about my own art. In these "*accidents,*" I know I was vital to the process, by allowing them to happen.

In learning to use all of your instincts when you paint, your reasons for painting become clearer and more identifiable.

Some guidelines for painting loose:

1. Follow the reason why you wish to paint

2. Sketch, even if you love abstraction

3. Welcome accidents—resist the conventional. Open up to it.

4. Try something irrational, like making the sky orange or

turning the painting upside down.

5. Paint daily with an attitude of play. This allows you to get more familiar with your tools.

6. Buy art supplies in bulk—so you don't worry about waste.

7. Carve out your own space and make it special for you. Even if it is a tiny room, set it up with music, candles or whatever will free your creative spirit.

Establish your own pattern of *mis en place* and stick to it. Once you get organized, you won't find any more excuses to put off your creative work and your journey will begin.

36" x 44" oil on canvas

Body Language

This huge painting started out as a play of yellow to red because I wanted to experiment with this combination. The shapes of the smaller couple came through immediately and I began to play off their interaction. I didn't especially want the intermingling of figures, but they called out to me. I answered. The front couple began to emerge. I added the play of pattern, suggesting furniture and buildings.

The painting told a story, hence, the name Body Language. The more one looks at the painting, the more of a story is told.

Sometimes, the inspiration for a painting is unknown until later. The daily routine of life plays a big part in my creativity. I have always been an observer of body language, instinctively reading when to interact or not. Being in the restaurant business trains you to observe and respond to people. Body language in a restaurant is fascinating.

I have also learned a lot about body language from the people who work manipulating bodies. I have a chiropractor whom I see regularly due to neck problems (work related, I am sure), and he is constantly noticing how body language reveals underlining physical problems. My friends, who give body massages agree. I notice the interactions with people more now that I understand body language.

Observe it for yourself. It may inspire you to paint, or write a short story or poem, or compose a piece of music. This piece is owned by Maxine Witt.

■

GOING WITH THE FLOW

Sometimes, when working, I experience a phenomenon

which is called "in the moment", otherwise known as "going with the flow." "Being in the moment" is when you experience maximum creative motivation and acute focus. This intense moment of living requires that the body and mind be in perfect unison. It is the joy of complete engagement. *Flow* tends to occur when a person's skills are fully mastered to overcome a challenge. For me, it is when I have pulled off a painting during a moment of intense living. It is about as perfect a moment as falling in love or having a child. It is the moment when your level of skill perfectly matches the degree of challenge presented. It is the same for a vocalist who is in full command of his/her vocal ability, or a surgeon performing an emergency operation with utmost skill.

My oldest son, who is a superior tennis player, once said he couldn't feel anything when he was playing "in the *flow.*" The harmony of his mind and body caused him to move effortlessly and play instinctively.

How does being "in the *flow*" work? By concentration and hours devoted to your craft. By complete immersion in feeling, thought and action. Only then will you gain control over your psychic energy, the basic fuel for creativity.

Being "in the *flow*" or "in the moment" eliminates all self-consciousness. Who you are and what you are doing become one. Only when it is over will the feeling of satisfaction and the rush of happiness occur. At that time, you can't wait to get it back.

The first time I experienced *flow* was in the middle of the night. I had been working on a poured acrylic painting and was having trouble finishing it. Suddenly, in the midst of a deep sleep, something occurred to me and I bolted out of bed, tore into the painting, finishing it while it was still dark! Totally exhausted, I went to bed and slept so soundly that I didn't notice I still had my artist's apron on, paint in

49

my hair, and paint on my face. The next morning, my husband said, "You look like you ate the painting!" After I cleaned up, dressed, and went back to my studio, I didn't recognize my painting. It had totally changed from what I remembered, but I was extremely excited about the outcome. I had remembered arising and working, but I had remembered neither the process nor the time involved. I had created a painting totally "in the moment"!

Winston Groom, a friend and author, once explained to me how the first chapter of one of his books was written in a moment of intense thought and inspiration. During a visit with his Dad, he heard a story about a simple man accomplishing something great, but in a humorous way, and his mind began to churn. Later that night, after leaving his Dad's house, he plunged into writing a story about just such a man, and before midnight, he had the first chapter finished. When Winston described how he had lost a sense of time and space in composing his story, I knew he had been "in the moment." The energy released from the inspiration and the clear vision of thought and action compelled him to excellence. That story was later entitled *Forrest Gump*. Winston told me that he'd always wanted to name a character "Gump" after the San Francisco department store, where he'd bought his first civilian clothes after returning from Viet Nam.

You cannot rationalize or intellectualize *flow*. You can only respect the possibility of your subconscious taking control at a time when your skill level is equal to your goal level. At that moment the creative energy generated from the harmony of inspiration and action is pure and uninhibited, and will often result in your best work. There are no bells or whistles to alert you. You just know! It's a lot like falling in love at first sight.

These eight elements further characterize *flow*:

1. There are clear goals every step of the way.

2. Action and awareness are merged.

3. There is a balance between challenges and skills. Skills are equal to the challenges.

4. There is immediate feedback by the doing. (In my case the actual painting tells me what to do next.)

5. There are no distractions. The subconscious takes over.

6. There is no worry or fear of failure.

7. Self-consciousness disappears.

8. The sense of time becomes distorted.

Creative people tell me that they experience *flow* in myriad and unexpected places, like swimming laps, sewing, driving or jogging. Patrick Grafton, author of *God's Royalty* had a key plot twist vision while washing his hair in the shower. With his eyes closed, the scenes and dialogue just sprang up. Lathered in soap, he called out for his wife, Diana, to bring a pad and pencil, and, while she sat on the edge of the adjoining tub, Patrick dictated the scene to her from behind his still closed eyes. Apparently, the soothing *flow* of warm water created a spasm of technicolor *flow*. Patrick also told me that he often has creative *flow* on solitary jogs around the countryside. Since his wife-scribe does not jog, he has learned to carry a small pad and pen in a jogging belly pack for those creative attacks. During one three-mile jaunt, he imagined the entire start-to-finish outline of a book. Later, Diana commented how she had witnessed *flow* from Patrick, but she couldn't rationalize or interpret *flow* for herself. "You need to be open to the possibility," I said.

Jog with the *flow*. Shower with the *flow*. Sew with the *flow*, but at all costs—go with the *flow*!

20" x 24" oil on canvas

Dance With Me

This is another example of a painting created in the moment of *flow*. It just happened! The more I understand *flow*, the more I can capture it. It is quite exciting to make a painting through the subconscious. I felt happy doing it and it floats like a dancer. So *Dance With Me!*

51

40" x 48" oil on canvas

The Party

This large oil was done so fast that I hardly remember the process. When color blocking and looking at the various shapes my brush and I made, I thought about how people at parties seem to resemble comic characters when they are engaged in the movement of conversation. Arms and legs move, cigarettes and glasses extend, and the festivity begins. I liked the element of a party in this painting. It is one of a series of five party paintings scattered all over the nation. Linda and Walter Greig of The Woodlands, Texas, own this one.

Resist the Conventional; Seek a Better Way.
Find it when you are ready.

This painting was actually two paintings. After three days, the first part of the painting was as much as you see now, without the suggestion of a body or a horizontal shape. I started with a blue palette and color blocking, and then had fun splattering with neutral diluted grayed down paint applied with a full brush dipped in

53

turpentine. The splattering idea came from an accident. I fell into the painting with a cup of turpentine. The accident was meant to be. Then I put the canvas away. I couldn't see what needed to be done to finish it. The painting rested in my studio for weeks. Patience is indeed a virtue, even when painting abstracts. Often a painting will speak back to you if you give it time. When I finally realized how to finish it, it only took two hours, thanks to *flow*. With the horizontal shape in place, it was clear how to strengthen the weak areas. Out of frustration came the satisfaction of completion. *The Shaman* went on to win a 1997 first place award in an "Artist of America" national show in Winston-Salem.

■

INSPIRING MINDS NEED TO KNOW!

Inspiration is elusive and fickle. It bestows its blessing on those who are open to it and sensitive to

their past and present experiences. To receive it you must open up your heart and mind to those people and feelings that touch your soul. For me, my children have been a great inspiration as well as nature, exotic trips, and the images of the *Masters of Art.*

I have been lucky enough to travel extensively, and meet all kinds of people. Wherever I've been lucky enough to go, those experiences have resurfaced as part of an inspired creative moment later in my work. That's how you use inspiration. You recreate a moment in time. It's what you get out of life's offerings. Even though travel is the best for learning and inspiration, you can gain inspiration from your circumscribed world or from the simplest moments. Remembering your child's first step, watching your husband put together a difficult toy for your son, receiving an album of remembrances from your mother, watching your child receive his Phi Beta Kappa honor and scholarship, running into an old friend, or just watching the fog slowly roll in from the sea.

When you are working at your best level, and are rewarded by inspiration, it's like a natural adrenaline high, and the more you *feel* life's moments as they evolve, the purer the inspiration.

Sometimes a smell can inspire. The scent of cookies baking, the marsh pluff mud, the aroma of clean laundry, or onions simmering. Friends create magical moments with a comfortable laugh during dinner, a shared memory, or a connection after a long lapse. I have painted paintings that are priceless to me because friends inspired them.

Part of the urge to create involves feeling things intensely and allowing yourself to be inspired by every emotion. The source of my

> *Observing the blank piece of paper in front of my child, I asked the question, "What are you drawing?"*
>
> *Tyson looked up, "I'm drawing a picture of God. Can't you see?"*
>
> *"But no one knows what He looks like," came my response.*
>
> *"Oh, but I'm not finished yet," he replied.*

55

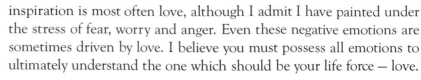

inspiration is most often love, although I admit I have painted under the stress of fear, worry and anger. Even these negative emotions are sometimes driven by love. I believe you must possess all emotions to ultimately understand the one which should be your life force — love.

You must strive to be in touch with your emotions— even pain, and use that pain to reach another level of understanding of yourself through the creative process.

A lot of us have our heads up our tu-tus, seeing narrowly, but when you come out of that narcissistic world, you can see everything as an outward and visible sign of inner grace. In order to receive inspiration, you must be open to it.

For me, personally. the simple moments in nature and with my family have inspired me: Watching nesting baby osprey fed by their mother near where our family was dining al fresco; seeing the majestic Bridal Veil Falls in Telluride, Colorado for the first time; listening to my youngest son humorously roast his Dad on a stage surrounded by friends; observing my oldest son exquisitely dancing the *Tango* with a beautiful partner; hiking up to the awesome rock formation of Delicate Arch, Utah with my family, just as the full moon rose through its arc; being served my favorite meal with champagne by my devoted husband my first night home with our infant child; and beating my male mates in a motor cross during a high performance driving course. The "rush" I had during those moments is the "rush" of inspiration. We must hold on to each golden moment and use it over and over again! **Life is sweet!! Express it!! Celebrate it!!**

One particularly inspirational encounter in my life occurred when my husband and I went to Bad Goisern, Austria, to meet Doctor Professor Frederich Neugebauer, a great artist and bookmaker.

It was December, 1987, and my husband Chris and I were in Berchtesgaden, Germany visiting his family, when we decided to call Professor Neugebauer and ask to meet him. He was a living legend in the art of calligraphy and bookmaking and his limited edition books had long inspired me. Although we were strangers, he graciously extended an invitation to visit his home, an hour and a half away. To our surprise, when we arrived, his charming wife had a feast waiting for us, and he offered us his personal Schnapps, which is indeed an Austrian sign of warmth and friendship. His obvious pride in a craft, which is rapidly declining in Austria, was evident when he showed us the carefully folded documents and papers of fine drawings and letter styles he'd mastered and designed during his initial five-year apprenticeship, a time he was especially proud of when he was still a hungry student.

Early in his career in graphics and printing, he was forced to fight in WWII, and was taken prisoner and spent four years in a crowded Egyptian detention camp with 10,000 other captives. Ironically it was there that he learned the necessary patience and stamina to begin his life's work in calligraphy design. Fashioning a writing instrument out of wood with the brush made from a friend's hair, he began to write on typing paper stolen from guards. For ink, he mixed medicine with sand and he created delicate letters and jewel like images that were museum quality.

"Today," he said, "it is only shown to eyes which appreciate its meaning."

Lovingly, he brought out each piece, preserved between plexiglass, and explained that when the English guard found the pages, he was so impressed that he let Dr. Neugebauer continue to do his work and kept it hidden from the other guards. In payment, Dr. Neugebauer made a book for him.

To think that these pieces were so perfectly crafted in such appalling life conditions brought tears to my eyes, and, when I looked up, Chris was wiping his eyes as well.

It touched us deeply that a man we had just met could open his heart to us and share stories of his life and art so freely. In the privacy of his workspace, he showed us his favorite tools which were the ones he had made himself out of sticks and bamboo with hand cut points. He painted only with turkey feather quills and wrote with the cured quills from the wing. He was, at this time, making limited edition books with his son on subjects that interested him. First he would read the work with a sense of the author's time and place in mind, then, before he put quill to paper, he would devote hours and hours of thought to each piece, deciding on the hand lettering, spacing, decorative detail and selected quotations. Each book reflected his personal feeling and interpretation of the essence of the work. Much as a sculptor sees the form living beneath a block of marble, waiting to be released, so Dr. Neugebauer envisioned how each work should appear on the naked page before he began.

He had a passion for all subjects, but the book that caught my eye was about nature and the beauty of rock forms. The letters were designed to resemble rocks and the rhythm of the book simulated the rush of brooks, and the abrupt obstacles of rock formations.

Ironically, when he needed money for his family, he couldn't sell his work, now he refuses most offers. I felt honored to come away with one of his creations.

Before leaving his workspace, he pulled out one last sheet of paper and carefully held it up for us to see.

"I bought this from a Jewish Torah maker over thirty years ago," he said. "It is the last true vellum made from an unborn calf. No more can be found. I am saving this last sheet for the perfect work." Reverently, he returned the vellum to its protective folder, and turned to me. "Now, I would like to see your work. You have brought something for me to see, I hope?"

In light of his extraordinary generosity, I couldn't refuse. Nervously, I placed two examples of my calligraphy on his desk and stepped back. He gazed at them for a long time, and then, to my relief, he turned to my husband and said — "A fine student of letters, and, one day a great master." At that, he winked at me and smiled his approval. It was more than I could have hoped for.

On the way home, I couldn't stop thinking about this simple, gracious man, who had truly lived his life according to his beliefs — a thinking man, an idealist, a purist. He hadn't driven a car for twenty years, because, as he put it — "It doesn't go with my state of mind."

To this day, I am moved by his passion and joy of life, and think often of his artistic purity when I am preparing to work.

Another inspiring encounter occurred when I was commissioned to transpose some poetry into calligraphy for the manager of a local radio station. When I arrived at the station with my 3-year old son in tow to pick up the poems, the secretary said, "Wait, he wants to see you in person," and ushered me into the manager's office. To my surprise, the young man remained seated, and, without looking up, motioned for me to sit, ignoring my son who was wandering after a Happy Birthday balloon.

After a long, awkward silence, he started to tell me the importance of this project and how he needed me to act quickly. Suddenly, he began to weep. Through tears, he explained that the author of these poems was his deceased fiancée who had been brutally murdered three weeks before. His whole body shook with pain.

Noticing his tears, my son wandered back to me and asked, as only a three-year-old can, "Why is the man crying, Mommy. Is he hurt?" At that, I broke down myself and somehow managed to say, "I know your pain. I have known it myself. I lost a special friend in an automobile accident. He was killed with his two best friends. I was supposed to be with them, but, by some twist of fate, I wasn't."

Quietly, my son went over to the man and said, "Don't cry, my Mommy will fix it!" We both managed to smile, dispelling the tension and grief in the room. It was the only time I thanked God for letting my child be there in the middle of an adult situation.

Pain inspires as deeply as joy. I threw myself into the project which resulted in a beautiful book and a healing for both of us.

Through it, he became a friend and special client. Three years later, I had the pleasure of designing his wedding invitations.

One final inspirational reminiscence involved a seven-foot charismatic pastor, who abruptly showed up at my studio to ask me to do some work for him. As he lumbered in, I must have looked very taken aback. Quickly, he said, "It is good to meet you my sister. I see you are suffering. Let me pray with you, and you shall be healed." I realized then that he must have noticed the brace on my hand, which the doctor had given me for carpal tunnel. We kneeled together and he prayed the most beautiful healing prayer I have ever heard. His deep, resonant voice moved me to tears. His name was Reverend Redish.

Although I had to wait for the doctor's permission to resume work, Reverend Redish's patience and prayer inspired me to appreciate both the work to be done and the rest needed to heal the injury. You never know when a client relationship will blossom into a friendship. You never know who may walk through your door, or what lessons you may learn from the moment. Keep your door and mind open. Meeting new and interesting people will inspire you and keep your work fresh.

> *Develop an interest in life as you see it; in people, things, literature, music; the world is so rich, simply throbbing with rich treasures, beautiful souls, and interesting people.*
> Henry Miller

30" x 30" oil on canvas

Spirit

Metmer Güler, a European painter whose show I attended, inspired this painting. I bought a small drawing of his at the show, along with his published book which was filled with photographs of colorful paintings which combined images with white paint scribbling in the shape of bodies. This interesting swirling of white paint is what inspired "Spirit". In it, I created a spontaneous burst of white shapes, which later suggested the feathers of an Indian headdress. The painting showed me my direction. It took control of the process. It guided my hand to produce areas of shape that I then could tap into and allow the painting to evolve intuitively. This painting has a unique "spirit" for me, like the artist who inspired it.

36" x 44" oil on canvas

The Secret

Here again, Metmer Güler's art influenced my work. His swirling, figurative mummy shaped white bodies inspired me to paint *The Secret*. My style of color block shapes came through again to create an interesting pattern, with an added illusion of a female figure to complement the painting. *The Secret* now tells a story, my story, of how inspiration connects one style of painting to another.

◼

A-Musing Voices

We all hear inner voices. Those voices are our intuitive response to what is happening around us. Few of us listen to those voices. Even fewer act on them, but to become creative you must learn to trust and make decisions, however zany, based on your own intuitive voices. Intuitive decisions are known as "gut level," "from the heart," "gestalt," or "leap of faith" decisions. They ignore society's predictable set of rules and regulations. They go "against the grain." They are "at odds." They are not easily made but are essential to finding your creative self.

When I talk about intuition, I am talking about the muse that speaks from my heart. The mention of my muse makes my children pat me on the head and murmur; "She's off again!" If I were not such a normal, community minded individual, people would think me a bit crazy, but instead they are just a bit a-mused.

My muse is the voice of my uncensored passion. It is that inner voice directing me toward who I am meant to be and what I am meant to do. Some people call this — God.

My intuition is what enables me to trust the heart-driven gut feeling instinct that tells me that what I am thinking of doing is right. Your intuition will give you power if you give it trust. Over the years, I have learned to trust my intuition when I paint or make a life decision.

We are all coded from within. We react intellectually, emotionally, intuitively, spiritually and physically. Some of us are left brained problem solvers, logically driven. Others are right brained, emotional beings, instinctively driven. Those of us who are spiritually driven as well feel we are a part of something greater than ourselves. All of these patterns of thought are related mostly to intuition, which can't be logically defined. We just have to trust the process.

When I was in my twenties, I impulsively swerved from one creative endeavor to another, much to my friends' and loved ones' dismay. I was doing everything from aerial photography, modeling, designing, to painting furniture, and working in marketing for a resort company. Painting and calligraphy were my hobbies. Even as I tried different things, I could hear this internally driven voice (the muse) telling me to do just one thing well, but it took me a long time to listen. I had a wild energy to tame. I was impulsively directed. I was excited and curious about life! Nothing got done as well as I intended. Becoming a mother and directing my energies toward my children forced me to slow down my creative exploration, but it also taught me the value of setting goals in pursuit of being an artist.

Ultimately, I had to choose one path of self-realization. Only then did the muse make any sense to me.

The muse is all that is good in your creative self, and it takes discipline and patience to harness it. Sometimes I resist the voice when I am struggling with a design project or a painting, and the muse says, "You're not in the right frame of mind; go play with your friends or husband, and come back another day." I may have a deadline, or a burning desire to continue, but I have learned that it is best to listen, or suffer with poor quality of work and poor peace of mind. Usually, if there is a deadline, somehow it gets done on time, following the inner voice's direction. Trust is the key.

You get confidence in your intuition by following it. It's like being in dancing school for the first time and hearing the teacher say, "Don't look at your feet, just dance!" You receive intuition when you quiet the rational mind, which tends to want to control and repress creativity.

Sometimes intuition is a little shy and needs a push. If you try not to crowd it or force it, it will come by gentle concentration. One must train oneself to hear that small voice. Children spontaneously hear it. You must find that ember of naiveté left in you and kindle it, for in that small flame your muse will rise and call out to you. If you get a message from your intuitive heart to get in touch with someone, go ahead and do it. If your intuitive heart says create something for someone now, do it. If you respond to the messages with action, you will be rewarded with positive, loving experiences.

People ask me what I do when I feel frustrated by the challenges of creativity. Usually, my answer is that I don't know all of the answers, but I do know this. When something is not working, try something different. Don't get bogged down. Make yourself try something more *complex* and daring. Your muse will help you. Just listen.

Sometimes problems are discovered during the process of creating a painting, because goals are not clear. Sometimes, the more *complex* the problem, the less clear it is what needs to be done. These problems become difficult to enjoy because their solutions are elusive. But I have learned to develop an unconscious mechanism, or sixth sense (intuition), which tells me what to do. This voice, or muse, summons you. You can't call on the muse whenever you wish. You can only be open and receptive to its call. The muse has your number — not you.

How do you learn to trust your intuition? By cultivating the curious and interested person in you who greets the world and life's experiences with openness. Try to be spontaneous and flexible in your approach to life. Keep processing events around you and incorporating them into your work, and you will begin to hear the voice within. Trust it. That is your *self* speaking. If you listen, your confidence will grow, and you will be able to accept whatever unexpected experience may be around the corner.

> *"No artist is truly pleased. There is [however] a queer, divine dissatisfaction, a blessed unrest that keeps us marching and makes us more alive than the others."*
> Martha Graham

> *"If I knew where I was going, I'd be lost"*
> Ron Prokrasso

42" x 36" oil on canvas

The Jester

This painting like so many others, started with blocks of color, and no plan. Slowly, a figure began to take shape. After a month long break from the painting, I went to the canvas again and knew intuitively how to shape the painting into an energetic, bouncing figure. As I balanced out the stripes to imply legs, arms, and a head, my mind was completely absorbed by the creative process. Every artist hopes for this power of concentration, but it doesn't always happen. When it does, the work is always effortless.

The Jester was completed in the summer after our local two-week arts festival in Charleston, S.C. called Spoleto USA. Undoubtedly, the costumes of the drama and opera inspired it. It won a top monetary award in the 1998 S.C. State Fair. It is now in the collection of Thayer Boswell Dodd of Mobile, Alabama.

■

ART-I-CHOKE

In my classes on creativity, there is always someone who

brings up the topic of being blocked creatively. I call this the Art-I-Choke state. This state of being is perfectly normal and it should not be feared. It is when your confidence level, your self-doubt, and your mind are closed all at once. So let it be closed! Let it be blocked! Let it be, period. There is a reason for this state to occur. Maybe something is going on in your life; a change or a growth period. This is a time to be open to a new and heightened awareness, by shutting down the old you. Give yourself permission to shut down. You must sometimes choke; you must sometimes be blocked in mind and spirit in order to grow. The Beatles song, Let It Be, captures this message about growth and acceptance. To its refrain I have added: Let go and let love.

"You have had the power all along," said the good witch to Dorothy.

"You just didn't know it."

As a creative person you must try to view the world with all of your senses heightened. Focus in new ways. Study other people and do not be threatened if their view of life may be bold and original. Establish your independence and approach life's obstacles and pitfalls with optimism and equanimity. Try to turn misfortune into an opportunity for growth and spiritual development. You can choose to be challenged or defeated. It's all in your attitude. Let it be. Let go and let love.

I have been "choked" many, many times. Writers call this being "blocked". Whatever it is, it's hard to understand. Each time I have experienced this, I have realized that memories are often the cause. Only when you confront old wounds and memories will you connect with life and its sometimes cruel reality. Luckily, I had great support at those times and learned a lot about myself and the importance of releasing emotional pain. I believe in sharing with others during an Art-I-Choke State of being. Go to someone you trust. Seek empathy and affirmations. Form a group of peers. Find someone with a big heart, one that has a pulse, not a timer. Be with people who enliven you. Do those things that make you glad to be alive.

Karen Weihs

Let it be. Let go and let love.

Throughout your life, you will experience these inactive periods, but new ideas and experiences will renew you and encourage growth. Your body will feel alive again and your mind voracious. Your creative soul is nourished by these voids. I call this the Art-I-Choke investigation and discovery period of creative growth. It is during this time one needs to learn how to surrender. Don't fight it. Don't protect yourself. Surrender! Something around you or inside you caused the chaos. You must work through the chaos bravely and strongly until the threat of being blocked goes away. This surrender doesn't eliminate the anxiety the first time or even the second, but each time it will be easier.

Let it be. Let go and let love.

Your conscious self is impatient for your success. Sometimes it wants to help you along so badly, it causes you to choke. When that happens, you try so hard it gets worse. Walking away from a frustrating situation when you want to do well is difficult. That is when you must rely on you subconscious, by letting go and not trying so hard. Tell your conscious self to stop hounding you with its pragmatic questions— When are you going to get started? What are you waiting for? When are you going to finish? What is your problem anyway?

Just tell it to shut up and go away and let your sub-conscious take over for a while. The subconscious is your friend.

Let it be. Let go and let love.

Consider the game of golf. It is a mental game like most sports. It is controlled by the conscious and unconscious mind. Painting is also a mental task, and like golf, it requires skill and patience. Golf and painting are about control and letting go at the same time. I have gotten disillusioned with golf and painting many times when my conscious self became too bossy. Once I went to my golf pro, Bobby Todd, for a lesson, because I was having problems with consistency. After watching me hit a few practice balls, he announced —"You are pushing the ball along with all your body, instead of your upper body. You are trying to force the ball along and consequently frustrating yourself and confusing your mind. You must not care so much. Let your subconscious control your muscle memory and RELAX. You haven't forgotten what you need to know, you've just overpowered it. Trust yourself!"

Bobby also made me hold the club with my fingertips instead of gripping it so hard. He forced me to let go and not try so hard. It worked. Later I confessed to him that I tell my students exactly the same thing — to relax and enjoy the process, rely on their skills and, if they keep working, their skill level will increase.

67

Let it be. Let go and let love.

In both golf and painting, I have choked each time I improved. You have to be patient and let your confidence catch up. It is a hard lesson to learn. I once watched a professional golfer choke on a ten-yard chip to lose the lead during the 1992 Ryder Cup at Kiawah's Ocean Course. In practice I am sure he made that shot a thousand times, but every attempt is different. Setting out on a course you've played many times is like facing the empty canvas. It's a completely new and different journey each time. In spite of tremendous skill, the mind can play frustrating games.

> "Golf like many professional tasks is a mental game of effortless power."
>
> Bobby Todd

Once, during a creativity talk at our gallery, a guest admitted her three-month Art-I-Choke State. She was a quilt designer, but she felt no desire to continue to design. She had moved to our state several months prior, and although she was settling in and making new friends, something was missing. She was conflicted about the move. She felt it was positive, but she just couldn't feel happy in her new home She couldn't concentrate and she felt lonely in her studio. She said she was distracted, rushing to do unplanned errands, fighting with her mother, wasting time in shopping malls, and worrying about the mole on her neck which looked stranger and stranger. This anxiety is common when you are blocked. The habit of perpetual distractions prevents the mind from being quiet enough to produce good work.

To arrive at silence you must invite silence in. You are the silencer and the silenced. Anxiety vanishes when the mind surrenders, and quiets.

> "Love is the spirit that motivates the artist's journey. The love may be sublime, raw, obsessive, passionate, awful, or thrilling, but whatever its quality, it is a powerful motive in the artist's life."
>
> Eric Maisel

For our new quilter friend, it was perhaps enough to feel that others understood her situation and that she was not alone. Many weeks after, she wrote to me that she'd created a new design and had broken through her creative impasse.

In my discussions with pupils, I have begun to understand the need for creative people to interact with other creative types. The best way to break the Art-I-Choke State-of-Mind is to talk with those who understand, slow down and be kind to yourself. Understand that fear and frustration are to be there when growth occurs. Your fears are really your muse's way to push you toward a creative break-through. Remember to let it be; let go, and let love.

One day I received a call from a man named Gil Hoffman who had seen my large abstracts and wanted to commission me to do two large pieces for his new Charleston apartment, overlooking the harbor. He invited me to see his place, and when we met, we instantly connected artist to client. Recently retired and divorced, he wanted to create a high style in his new apartment. He wanted his east view of the river and the three-mile Cooper River Bridge on one wall, and his south view of the Battery on the other large wall of his living room. As soon as I got home, his enthusiasm and confidence inspired me to work. From then on, he called me daily to check on the progress. At first, I was flattered by his telephone calls, but then, his participation began to impede my progress. I felt "blocked". I began to question, "What if I cannot measure up to his expectations?" I explained my doubts to him, and told him of my confusion with our artist/client relationship. His response was just what I needed to hear. "Just do it with all your power," he said. "I'll check you in two weeks. You'll do it!"

I finished the project to his satisfaction, and to mine. My own honesty had inspired me. He later insisted that I enter the painting in the competition for the city's annual 10K Cooper Bride Run poster. I did, and it won! Posters of the painting were made. When Gil remarried and moved to Florida, he brought the painting back to me, since he had no large walls. I still have the painting today; and he has a poster. He visits his painting occasionally, but he has no intentions of asking it back from me. He feels I should have it as a reminder of my leap in confidence. What a guy!

22" x 18" oil monotype

Passages

This monotype (an oil painting on glass, transferred to paper by pressing the glass into the paper using an etching press) was an attempt at combining colorful shapes and scribbles of calligraphy to

70

create an interesting design. Later, I applied more calligraphy strokes, using colorful pencils, crayon d'arche, and ink. I love to do monotypes. It utilizes all of my skills: drawing, painting, and calligraphy. I studied calligraphy for years, and I do not plan to abandon my long dedication to it. My training as a calligrapher anchored my painting, taught me patience, and a good design sense. The name of this painting is an homage to all the phases of my creative growth.

14" x 14' oil monotype

Momentum

This monotype illustrates most of my skills in design, painting, and lettering. The loose lettering on the finished surface of the monotype breaks all of the rules of professional calligraphy. I had to learn the rules of lettering and design before I successfully defied them. The strength of letter making is determined by the circular letter shaping combined with the straight edge of the initial design. Loose lettering begins with the proper knowledge of good lettering but is expressed with a confident fast stroke. I tell my students to take a piece of scrap paper first, close their eyes, and feel the stroke while making it. Then repeat it on the design piece." (Maybe have a glass of wine, first.) Confidence comes with the knowledge of design and shape and, the use of proper tools and practice, practice, practice. Empower yourself with knowledge! Learn all you can and don't stop being a student. In order to become a good teacher, you must keep learning by being a student yourself.

"Momentum" won the honor of being published in the fall of 1995 Letters Arts Review magazine. The editor liked the art/lettering combination and had me write about its conception.

46" x 42" oil on canvas

Gnarled

This piece is both realistic and expressionistic. It depicts the gnarled shapes of beach trees blown by years of directional wind. The repetitive, time-ravaged misshapen trees instantly attracted me. At sunset, I can really see their shapes. This piece was simple in its inception, but complicated in its outcome. Its moody image is deliberate. When I do a more realistic piece, I always like to dramatize the subject with an expressive background. This green to blue to midnight blue sky conveys, through abstract patterns, the drama of a southern sunset.

My youngest son, Justin, didn't believe our southern skies ever changed to green until he saw it for himself one late afternoon while he was driving home from the beach. He thought I made it up! He was so excited to confirm my observation. He's developing his own artist's eye through mine.

ART-I-FACT

Throughout this book,

I have talked about a number of techniques and attitudes that can help you discover and nurture your creativity. I call them Art-I-Facts, because they have been passed down — artist by artist through the years, both consciously and unconsciously, much as "artifacts" representing an ancient way of living. If you observe and practice them, you will certainly uncover your creative self in whatever way you choose to express it.

The best time to dance is when the music is playing.

As Art-I-Facts, they also represent the facts or the truth about how to lead a more creative life as I see them. The facts of art as interpreted by me — Art-I-Facts. Your interpretation will reflect your own sense of Art-I-Facts for you. It is personal and unique to each one of us.

Everything happens at the time it should.

You will undoubtedly add some of your own Art-I-Facts, but the essential ones remain:

Face the negative and replace it.
Use your artist brain and believe in the, "Yes I can" attitude.
Value your work and write a mission statement about it.
$A + I + S + G \times T = Success.$
Celebrate your dichotomy.
Practice Mis en Place.
Work out of your mind — "in the flow".
Listen to your muse for inspiration.
Let it be, let go and let love.

In this intense, hustle-bustle world, it is difficult to quiet your mind, but you must, if you want to create. Only when your mind has quieted to the outside world can you open it to your inner voice. Each of us has our own way of finding that quiet. Some go to a museum or simply sit and reflect. Some meditate or take a long walk. Some enjoy a movie or read a good book. Whatever it may be, you must do it. Only when you quiet your mind will the ideas come, and only when you open it, will those ideas have a chance of connecting.

Dr. Eric Maisel named this practice the *hush and hold* theory in his book, *Fearless Creating*. He says out of this hushing of the mundane world come ideas and visions. Out of this state come all the world's symphonies, songs, paintings and business trends. But the idea must be held. The outer world feeds your inner world and then you must hurry away and nurture each new idea in the seclusion of creativity. It's an Art-I-Fact.

One friend of mine who is a doctor goes to sit in an abbey in Moncks Corner, S.C. every Friday so he can hush and hold his mind. He finds it as necessary to do as playing golf with his buddies or partying with his old college friends. It's a ritual that helps him gain perspective on his life and work.

I go to a stream on our property in the mountains of North Carolina. There I hear the rushing of the water as I hush and hold. It's there I reach into my soul and find my spirit.

If your idea is a valid one and your mind is quiet, you will discover that you are suddenly not wishing to create, but are creating. If you're afraid of being alone, frightened of your own quiet, frightened of what you'll find when you hush and hold, you must work on loving yourself more and making solitude a safer and less scary place. In the quiet, your creative spirit will awaken. In the quiet you will hear the music playing, and begin to dance.

My friend, Sue, and I read the "dance when the music is playing" quote on a wall at a country music club in downtown Charleston, South Carolina when we were there with a group of friends learning to line dance. Several of us went weekly, not only to have fun, but also to support Sue, who had cancer. She always wanted to learn line dancing. It was one of the best and saddest times of my life. We made a night of it and our group got larger and stronger as our enthusiasm grew. Sue was a highly creative person who knew how to charm everyone into enjoying themselves. She was an excellent faux finisher and decorative arts inventor. Her special talent for her friends was picking gifts and treats to fit any occasion, and then telling stories to go along with them.

When Sue's condition worsened and she couldn't dance any longer, we convened at her home, told stories, and watched movies until she tired of us. Our good times line dancing during her last days will stay with me always. She died happy, but way too young. I have always remembered that sign and I try to live by it. Sue danced creatively her whole life because she heard the music playing, just like the quote says, right up until the "last call".

Life is a constant state of change and motion, which eventually will end. We are all terminal. We are born and we will die. All that we have created will crumble. If you approach life as if all is ephemeral, you will cease to be afraid of creating. Your attitude will be positive and your philosophy will be a metaphor for let it be, let go and let love. To find your own personal balance, you must relax, be flexible to change and think of what you have, instead of what you want. You will get what you want by appreciating what you already have — a brain, desire, the goal of learning. You will get what you want by practicing what you've learned with a positive attitude. Then what you already have will become richer.

I always keep my first drawings around to look at when negative thoughts creep in. It's pretty awful to look at them, but they remind me of what I've achieved, and the value of each step along the way. In my early years as an artist, many times I felt insecure. It's okay to feel frightened, even a little jealous, greedy or angry in the beginning. Rather than bury your feelings, open up to them, move through them until you no longer think of your negative feelings as a big deal. When you are open to the totality of your life, you no longer have to pretend or hope that your life is perfect and acceptable to everyone. You can accept yourself as you are right now. Then you can feel free and open to each new experience.

One of my teachers once admired a drawing I did and then said, "Now tear it up and do it again." Saddened, I did as I was instructed, and to my surprise, the piece was better than before. That taught me to trust the process and keep working.

Two years ago, I had an emergency operation and had to be inactive for a few months. Two discs herniated in my neck causing paralysis in my right arm. The auto accident 10 years prior coupled with work related habits were the culprits. I decided to make the best of my idle time and began journaling. When I looked over my thoughts and my teaching notes, ideas began to fall into place — ideas for this book. Rather than going out of my mind with pain and inactivity, I lay on my den sofa and wrote about being *Out of My Mind.*

There is vitality, a life force, energy, a quickening that is translated through you into action and because there is only one of you in all time, this expression is unique. And, if you block it, it will never exist through any other medium and will be lost.

Martha Graham

The essence of your creative spirit is found in the child you once were. It is not gone, it has merely fallen asleep and been shut away behind many large doors marking the passages of maturity. What you must do is find the keys to those doors and unlock them, one by one until you enter the last chamber and gently shake your inner child awake.

That pure and unselfconscious spirit is difficult to describe and believe in. I often explain spirit to my students with a story about my son. His spirit has always been apparent in his verbalization. I signed him up once for violin lessons, acting lessons and tennis lessons when he was nine. When I told him of his schedule, he said, "Mom! Don't sign me up! I don't want to be signed up. I'll tell you when I want to be signed up." His spirit was talking to me. It was telling me not to encroach. He had his own agenda.

Now as a young man, he continues to express his creativity by writing lyrical and comedic material. I have learned a lot about spirit from children. The secret is to keep that spirit alive as an adult. The "Don't Sign Me Up" attitude shows spirit.

Seek your inner child, which is a little naïve, a little irresponsible, a little exuberant, and a lot passionate. Be open and aware with enough of a balanced ego to let go and let love. We are all occupying the same space, but on different levels. Following your spirit puts you on the highest level. It's an Art·I·Fact.

Hush and hold, listen for your music and follow your inner spirit. You have nothing to lose by trying, and everything to lose by denying. Take everyday for what it is, a gift, and the opportunity to be creative as only you can. Living with spirit will define you as a life artist.

9" x 14" gouache on paper

Just Do It

This calligraphic piece tells all! A Frenchman first used this phrase, then the Japanese coined it, and we Americans know it well from the advertising of Nike Sports. Whoever said it first, the meaning is profound and honest ... Attack life! However mundane or exciting your life may be, let it passionately reflect who you are. Whatever you decide to do, Just Do It. Just Do It with confidence!

■

ART OFFICIAL
ABOUT THE ARTIST

Karen Weihs, a native of Charleston, South Carolina, graduated from the University of Georgia and has been a professional artist since an early age. Beginning her career as a graphic designer for a resort corporation, she then progressed into freelance graphic design, winning many state awards. After much study, she became a Master Calligrapher, developing a line of prints that are still sold nationally to the gift market industry. In 1995, Karen helped found the Waterfront Gallery in Charleston, S.C., a highly successful artist's co-operative She has won many state and national painting awards. Painting, teaching and lecturing are now her life's work.

My artwork is constantly growing and changing. My approach is expressive, emotional, and intuitively creative. It reflects me as well as my attitude about life.

As a wife, mother of two boys, and businesswoman, Karen has learned to be creative in every facet of her life. She has begun to bring her message of creativity to people in diverse professions.

Sharing my ideas about creativity with people who don't consider themselves creative has been the most rewarding. By the end of my seminar, they're full of ideas and raring to go. It's inspiring.

Consistent with the duality of a creative soul, Karen resides both in Charleston, S.C. and Cashiers, N.C.

The air in the mountains of N.C. and the ocean breezes of coastal S. C. both bring energy into my work as an artist. The serenity of the mountain life is a great escape from the city, but the charm of Charleston and its people hold my heart.

I feel I am ready to work out of my mind anytime I become inspired. It may be a phone call from a friend that inspires me or a student or just a vista that intrigues me while walking my two Boykin spaniels. The principles of creative power, which I've learned to embrace, enrich my spirit instinctively.

Who am I now?

I am responsible, but don't want to be.
I am smart, but naiveté beckons me.
Bound to tradition, yet seduced by fantasy,
I create my life around inspiration.
Beauty abounds around me.
The world is steeped with amazement and wonder.
I tackle it with laser beam direction.
But exhausted by its attraction,
I rest and am rejuvenated once again.
Passion propels me,
then objectivity blankets me.
Paradoxes prevail—
perpendicular poles of personality.
Normal?
I question if I am.
Or genius?
I feel like a spark kindled by a culture
Fueled by fickle and kind.
I live from pain,
exposing anxiety.
I suffer to demonstrate
the sensitivity of my soul.
But I gain such joy.
Shy and self-deprived—
then remarkably self-assured,
I struggle with my own determination
quite aware of a world's contribution.
I want to matter.
I want to show love.
I feel like—
I am,
A multitude in my own
individuality.

Karen Weihs